PRIVATE AND SECRET

PRIVATE AND SECRET

*The Clandestine Activities of a
Nineteenth-century Diplomat*

Robert Franklin

Book Guild Publishing
Sussex, England

First published in Great Britain in 2005 by
The Book Guild Ltd
25 High Street
Lewes, East Sussex
BN7 2LU

Typesetting in Times by
Acorn Bookwork Ltd, Salisbury, Wiltshire

Printed in Great Britain by
CPI Bath

A catalogue record for this book is available from
The British Library.

ISBN 1 85776 972 4

Contents

Preface

Charles Stuart, Lord Stuart de Rothesay, is a minor but not insignificant figure in British diplomatic history; he was certainly neither an insignificant nor an uninteresting man. It is surprising, therefore, that relatively little has been written about him. He has always had a place in the Dictionary of National Biography, but he is mentioned only in passing in history books and memoirs, except in Violet Stuart Wortley's volumes of family history, *A Prime Minister and His Son*, *Highcliffe and the Stuarts* and *Magic in the Distance*, none of which is a full biography. It was work on a history of St Mark's Church, Highcliffe, Christchurch, which he built, that introduced me to him, and my biography, *Lord Stuart de Rothesay*, was published in 1993. There were many references in his papers to his clandestine activities, but it was feedback from readers of the biography that made a separate account of these activities seem worthwhile.

This book would not have been written if Barbara Abbs had not told me what she knew about Charles Stuart's servant William Wood, and supplied me with references, or if Elizabeth Sparrow's study of the work of British agents in France during the French Revolutionary and Napoleonic Wars, *Secret Service*, had not appeared when it did; it might not have been published if it had not been for the encouragement of Dr Brendan Simms of Peterhouse, Cambridge, who took the trouble to comment on the manuscript in detail. I am particularly grateful to two other private individuals: Lord Joicey, for his transcription of Charles Stuart's first travel journal; and my former colleague Mr James Bramble FRCS, for his opinion on a surgical question discussed in the chapter on Queen Caroline.

I want to thank the archivists, librarians and others who have given me help and advice at the Bodleian Library,

Oxford, the British Library, Buckinghamshire Record Office, Cambridge University Library, the Codrington Library at All Souls College, Oxford, Coutts & Co.'s Archive, East Sussex Record Office, Edinburgh University Library, the Hallward Library at the University of Nottingham, the Hartley Library at the University of Southampton, Highcliffe Castle, the National Archives at Kew, the National Library of Scotland, the Rothschild Archive and the West Yorkshire Archive Service. Melanie Aspey, Director, The Rothschild Archive, was kind enough to go through the chapter on the Rothschilds and make corrections.

I have had the kind permission of the Earl and Countess of Harewood and Trustees of the Harewood House Trust to quote from the Canning Papers. Others I have to thank specifically for permission to make quotations are:

Spellmount Publishers Ltd, The Village Centre, Staplehurst, Kent, for permission to quote from *Intelligence Officer in the Peninsula*, by Julia V Page.

The Random House Group Ltd, for permission to quote from *Magic in the Distance*, by Violet Stuart Wortley, published by Hutchinson.

I regret that I have not been able to trace the holders of the copyrights of *A Prime Minister and His Son* and *Highcliffe and the Stuarts*, by The Hon Mrs Edward (Violet) Stuart Wortley, *The Rise of the House of Rothschild*, by Count Corti, and *Rothschild – A Story of Wealth and Power*, by Derek Wilson. I should be pleased to hear from them.

Robert Franklin
Christchurch, 2005

1

Early Influences 1779–1801

There are several existing likenesses of Charles Stuart, Lord Stuart de Rothesay, but the portrait by François Gérard at the Victoria and Albert Museum seems to reveal something about him that the others do not. It shows him alert but detached, and looking straight at whatever is in front of him as if he is taking everything in and giving nothing away. He is wearing a cloak, and he is holding a pair of gloves that could easily be imagined to be a dagger. If nature and nurture, together, made him what he was, certain early influences may have been particularly important in this respect.

Charles Stuart, later 1st Baron Stuart de Rothesay, was born in 1779.[1] His paternal grandfather, John Stuart, 3rd Earl of Bute, was one of the two Secretaries of State in the days when those great functionaries controlled the country's Secret Service, chiefly through the agency of the Post Office.[2] As Prime Minister, Lord Bute's greatest achievement was to bring the Seven Years' War to an end, and he is reputed to have done so by bribing Members of Parliament from secret funds.[3] Charles' father, General Sir Charles Stuart, a distinguished soldier, could not rely on official sources for intelligence; the Army had no intelligence service, as such, until 1803, when the Depot of Military Knowledge was set up;[4] and he learned to provide for himself.

The elder Charles first saw active service in the American War of Independence, in which he must have become familiar

1

with the ways and means of intelligence-gathering that were found in that conflict. It is a conflict that figures largely in the history of military intelligence for the exploits of Major John André, Adjutant General to the British Army and chief intelligence officer to the Commander-in-Chief, General Sir Henry Clinton.[5] Colonel Stuart, as he then was, and General Clinton were in each other's confidence, and Stuart is unlikely to have been ignorant of the sort of work that André was doing. Clinton certainly wrote to Stuart, who was by then at home in England, with the news, when André was eventually captured and executed as a spy.[6]

In the years between the American War of Independence and the French Revolutionary War, he was left unemployed, but he did not leave himself unoccupied. He spent several years, in total, travelling in Europe, at first apparently simply showing a soldier's interest in military matters, but later, in 1787, certainly collecting military and political intelligence, which he transmitted, anonymously and through an intermediary, to Lord Hawkesbury, President of the Board of Trade.[7] Hawkesbury, as Charles Jenkinson, had been Lord Bute's protégé and he was acting at this time in some respects as Stuart's patron; he was a man with many contacts in governmental and royal circles, and there can be no doubt that he passed on the information that he received from Stuart to the relevant authorities.

As General Stuart, he turned the French out of Corsica in 1794, organised the defence of Portugal in 1797 and captured Minorca in 1798, unfortunately, but perhaps not surprisingly, leaving few records of what he did or was done in his name in the intelligence field in these years. One of the stories told by Violet Stuart Wortley, however, suggests that he took full advantage of an acquaintanceship made in Corsica with Philippe Masseria, friend and confidant of the Corsican patriot Paoli. Mrs Stuart Wortley was writing of the negotiations that preceded the Peace of Amiens in 1801:

2

In the meantime the ground had been unofficially explored through the instrumentality of a Corsican, Captain Masseria, of the Corsican Artillery, whose qualifications for the mission consisted in his intimacy with the Bonaparte family, dating back to the days of mutual struggle in their native island. Masseria had been used as a secret agent by General Stuart, and by him introduced to his nephew, Lord Hobart, for work of a confidential nature.[8]

Lord Hobart was Secretary of State for War and the Colonies.

General Stuart's task in Portugal was to assist in the defence of the country against Spain, acting as an agent of France; it was complicated by the confused state of political and military affairs in Portugal, and by lack of clarity in his instructions from the then Secretary of State for War, Henry Dundas. To make matters worse, he had under his command a body of French refugees, some members of which had divided loyalties. Good intelligence must have been vital to him, and a letter from Lord St Vincent, at sea off the coast with his fleet, suggests that he was well served in Spain.

I return you a thousand thanks for an interesting letter by the *Sea Horse* with the accurate intelligence from Galicia; your spy in that quarter seems as intelligent as the one at Badajoz.[9]

St Vincent described Stuart to Dundas as 'the best Lieutenant-General you have'.[10]

Young Charles was at Eton until he was 16, in 1795, and he went up to Christ Church, Oxford, in 1797. Violet Stuart Wortley tells us that his father sometimes took him with him on his travels while he was still a schoolboy,[11] and we have his own account of the two years between Eton and Christ Church in a journal, *Travels in Germany and the Imperial Hereditary*

3

States, 1795–1797.[12] This journal is as interesting for what it tells us about him as for the travelogue itself, though probably because he was writing for others rather than himself it is disappointingly impersonal: he was evidently an observant and resourceful young man; he was certainly already a bibliophile. At Weimar he sat at the feet of Goethe and Schiller, and penned descriptions of these great men of letters.

The content of the journal would have been unlikely to raise suspicions in the minds of censors in any of the countries through which he passed, but his letters to his father, by then in Portugal, are another matter. He wrote from Weimar on 10 June, 1797:

> Everything in this country has a very war-like appearance though few people seem to know how it will turn out. The whole Saxon Army has received orders to hold themselves in readiness to march at a moment's notice. The Emperor has formed a camp of 60,000 men near Olmutz, upon the Prussian border. Luchesini the Prussian minister is gone back to Berlin, and the Prussians are exceedingly busy in fortifying all their frontier places towards Galicia in the newly acquired part of Poland. Some people say war is declared; I must confess it appears to me very odd that the House of Austria should take such a step after being so weakened as she certainly has been in the French war.[13]

His travels left him restless. After a year at Oxford, he moved to Glasgow University; then, in 1799 he set out with a party of fellow students, which included Henry Brougham, the future Lord Chancellor, on a sailing expedition. This was to have taken them to the Western Isles and on to Iceland, but storms forced them to abandon the second half of the voyage, and Charles and Brougham planned, instead, a tour of Scandinavia and Russia. They were disappointed again, however, because Charles was called back from Stockholm by his father, who was putting his affairs in order in preparation for a return to active service. But General Stuart was ill and he died in 1801, without having seen any more fighting.

Charles had already been admitted to Lincoln's Inn, and he began to read for the Bar, but he was still unable to settle. He considered politics and proposed himself as Member of Parliament for Poole, in Dorset, a borough that his father had represented for many years, but he was given no encouragement in Dorset or at Westminster. Then nepotism asserted itself, and Lord Hobart found him a place in the Diplomatic Service. He was to be Secretary of Legation at Vienna; but he had time to spare, and he decided that now was his chance to see something of Russia. It was the summer of 1801, and Europe was in a state of suspended animation: the French Revolutionary War was over, but the Peace of Amiens had not yet come into being.

The Second Coalition against France had crumbled, and England was alone. Her security depended on her Navy and the trade that the Navy guaranteed, but her supremacy at sea was challenged by the so-called Armed Neutrality of Denmark, Sweden, Prussia and Russia, aided and abetted by France. In April 1801, however, Nelson destroyed the Danish fleet at Copenhagen, and Denmark's allies, already shaken by the assassination of Tsar Paul, backed down. The Swedish fleet, at Revel, and the Russian fleet, at Kronstadt, were also to have been attacked, and they might have been destroyed likewise, but they happened to be protected by thick ice.

Charles set out at the beginning of July, and travelled through Prussia, staying briefly in Berlin, through partitioned Poland, staying briefly in Warsaw, and through Russia as far as St Petersburg, where he stayed for two weeks. Then he turned back, through Russian Poland and Austria to Vienna, where he arrived at the end of September. He kept a journal again, *Journal, Northern Europe 1801*,[14] and this time he recorded what he saw and heard as a budding diplomat rather than a student or the dutiful son of a British officer. There are copious notes on political, economic and military matters, and there is an interesting reference to a visit to Kronstadt. He remarked that some of the attractions of St Petersburg were not on the tourist trail and went on:

> Cronstadt [*sic*] was the only object of this kind I visited during my residence here, and that rather from motives of curiosity to see the preparations they had made to resist the attack of our fleet in case it had come to that port. We went down the river, which was at this time crowded with vessels, but could not but smile at the trifling works which had been erected, and the evident acknowledgement of the people that they were insufficient for the purpose intended.[15]

Kronstadt may have been the only object of the kind in question on his itinerary, but it is unlikely that he visited this island fortress and naval base solely from motives of innocent curiosity. He made notes on all that he saw there.

2

Introduction to the Diplomatic Service 1801–1804

In 1782, the duties of the two Secretaries of State, including the control of Britain's rudimentary Secret Service, which had been shared hitherto, were divided between home affairs and foreign affairs, and the offices of Home Secretary and Foreign Secretary were established.[1] The nerve-centre of the Secret Service was the Post Office, which collected and transmitted information through its well-developed communications network, obtaining much of its most valuable information by intercepting letters.[2] Foreign correspondence was handled in the so-called Secret Office, for which the Foreign Secretary became responsible.[3]

The existence of the Secret Office was never officially acknowledged or betrayed, and its reports were passed to ministers on a 'need to know' basis. Foreign governments were well aware of what was going on, however, and they did the same themselves. Letters to or from other countries, particularly those to or from diplomats, were intercepted, opened, scanned for invisible ink, copied and, if necessary, deciphered and translated. They were then given counterfeit seals and sent on their way. An added refinement of the process was the forgery of false information, which could be 'planted'.

Ten years later, in 1792, when the French Revolution was in full swing, Parliament gave London, outside the City, a police force and stipendiary magistrates, to maintain law and order and, more specifically, to take action against anyone suspected of subversive activities. The powers of the magistrates to deal with foreigners (more specifically, suspicious visitors from France) were augmented in the next year, 1793, and an Alien Office was set up to organise surveillance. Some magistrates now found themselves expected to conduct confidential or secret enquiries, and certain of them showed an aptitude for such work, prominent among these being William Wickham.

Gradually, the Alien Office became a Secret Service office, its work complementing that of the Secret Office.[4] Although the Foreign Secretary was responsible for the Secret Office and the Home Secretary was responsible for the police, the magistrates and the Alien Office, the convention was that the Foreign Secretary took precedence in Secret Service matters; and the convention was observed the more faithfully during this period, the second period of William Pitt's first administration, from 1794 to 1801, for the fact that the Foreign Secretary, Lord Grenville, and William Wickham were old friends.

Wickham was made Superintendent of Aliens, and as such head of the Alien Office, in 1794; and later in that year he was sent abroad on a secret mission. Grenville had received a request from certain private individuals in Switzerland for help in mounting a counter-revolution in France, and it was necessary to check on the credentials of these men. The occasion was a notable one in two respects: it marked the introduction of a doomed policy of supporting royalist counter-revolutionaries; it also marked the emergence of what came, in due course, to be known as Her (then 'His') Majesty's Foreign Secret Service.[5]

Grenville and Wickham and their respective successors continued to work through the Secret Office and the Alien Office, and when Wickham was made Chief Secretary in Ireland, in 1802, he probably made use of the Irish Office in London in the same way.[6] The Duke of Portland became involved with the Secret Service when he joined Pitt's administration as Home Secretary in 1794, and he provided some continuity of oversight and control in successive administrations, including his own, until his death in 1809. Counter-revolution in France was fostered when opportunity arose, but the infiltration and manipulation of sections of the French government and the French Army came to be seen as a better option.[7]

The Foreign Office and the Diplomatic Service were separate organisations until as late as 1918,[8] but they worked together, and the King's ministers abroad, like his ministers at home, were supplied with the intelligence that they were considered to need to know; and the traffic in intelligence was two-way. Diplomats set up their own intelligence operations, or, at least, found their own agents and sources. Naturally, they said little and recorded less of these operations, but references to some of them can be found in their papers, their private correspondence always being more revealing in this respect than their official dispatches.

The three years that Charles spent at Vienna – 1801 to 1804 – coincided, more or less, with the Peace of Amiens and the premiership of Henry Addington. As Secretary of Legation he had a difficult role to play, if only because it was ill-defined; though he would have been recognised as a future minister and ambassador, and he was Chargé d'Affaires, in the absence of his minister, Sir Arthur Paget, from August 1803 to March 1804.[9] He was answerable to Paget in the first instance and then to the Foreign Secretary, Lord Hawkesbury, and it would have been part of his duty to report on intelligence matters to them, but he also reported regularly to Lord Hobart. The nature of his responsibility to Hobart is not clear, but he provided the Secretary of State for War with a continuous flow of intelligence.[10]

Addington stood for peace and a reduction in government expenditure, and one of his first acts as Prime Minister was to reduce expenditure on the Secret Service, which may have been a false economy. He and his Cabinet colleagues did their best to persuade themselves that peace between Britain and France was possible, and that generous concessions were worth making in order to achieve it, arguing that they had been given a safe fallback position by the Treaty of Lunéville. This treaty, between Austria and France, provided for the transfer to France of the left bank of the Rhine but recognised the independence of Holland, Switzerland and northern Italy. Such self-deception became increasingly difficult, however, in the face of military posturing and diplomatic manipulation on the part of Napoleon.

The future of Malta was a particularly contentious issue, and one in which Charles had a special interest. France had taken the island from the Knights of St John, and when, in 1800, Britain had taken it from France, Charles' father had been instructed to superintend its return to the Knights, who, by this time, had placed themselves under the protection of the Tsar. But General Stuart had declined to have anything to do with this arrangement, on the grounds that Malta deserved better; he described the Knights as 'the most corrupt, hypocritical and cowardly vagrants that ever were fostered', and referred to the Tsar in terms that were scarcely more complimentary.[11] Malta was thus, at this time, still in Britain's hands.

Charles' reports to Lord Hobart ranged widely in a geographical sense, but they were particularly concerned with the Italian states. Each of the several states in the north of the country was already under Napoleon's influence in some way, and all were, therefore, vulnerable to his schemes of aggrandisement. What was more, as Charles noted in one of his reports, on 27 June 1802,[12] Britain then had no diplomatic or consular representation in the peninsula, except at Naples, in the south. All this meant that there was a major trouble spot in Europe of the affairs of which the British government's sources of information were unusually limited; but Austria's geographical and historical links with the area made Vienna a useful intelligence post, and Charles made the most of it.

The Cisalpine Republic, a state recently established at the pleasure of France, with Milan as its capital, bowed to the inevitable and accepted the suzerainty of Napoleon; and then, with certain accretions, was renamed the Italian Republic. In the Republic, Charles reported ominously, on 31 October 1802,[13] large numbers of men were being enlisted and large amounts of military supplies were being ordered. Shortly afterwards, the Duchy of Parma was absorbed into it, and if *force majeure* was one factor in this development another was the convenient death of the Duke of Parma. 'This sudden event', Charles told Hobart, writing from Vienna as usual, 'is here openly stated to be the consequence of poison'.[14]

Piedmont, the mainland half of the Kingdom of Sardinia-Piedmont, had already allowed itself to be absorbed into France, while the island of Sardinia was protected by the Royal Navy. Charles informed Hobart, in his report of 31 October 1802, that pressure from Piedmont was being brought to bear on its neighbour, the Ligurian Republic, based in Genoa, to do likewise. [15] The remaining states of the north, the Kingdom of Etruria, that is Tuscany, and the Papal States, were no more than satellites of France. According to Charles, in the same report, military preparations in the Italian Republic and other states of the north boded ill for Switzerland.

Switzerland, as the Helvetic Republic, had been another of France's satellites, and its confederation of independent states had had union imposed on it. However, under the terms of the Treaty of Amiens, French troops were withdrawn. Representatives of the old states then demanded a return of their old independence, and led a revolt against the central government in order to obtain it. There was no doubt that France would support the central government, and the insurgents appealed for the help of other nations. Britain was ready, as ever, to provide subsidies but, for obvious logistical reasons, could not provide men. Paget was instructed to suggest that Austria should send in troops, and a British agent, known as Mr Moore (whether or not this was really his name) was sent to Switzerland to rally the insurgents and to explain Britain's position.

Paget soon discovered that no help was to be expected from Austria, and he sent Charles to meet Moore at Constance and give him this bad news. Charles was bound to report back to Paget on this mission, but he wrote to Hobart about it, too: 'As I take it for granted you have perused Mr Moore's dispatches at the Office', he said in a letter of 14 December 1802, 'I shall not swell this letter with a precis of the various information I brought Mr Paget'.[16] He made a point of adding, however, presumably because there was some significance in it, that he had spent several days with Moore and a certain Swiss general, and that he had travelled back to Vienna through northern Switzerland, the Tyrol and Salzburg.

Whatever instructions Paget had given Charles, the mission to Switzerland had involved more than the delivery of an update by a young and inexperienced diplomat to an agent in the field: the diplomat and the agent had been collecting intelligence. But nothing that Britain could do was to alter the fate of Switzerland. France decided what should be done, as self-appointed mediator between the insurgents and the central government. A sort of confederation was the result, but it was not the old confederation of independent states for which the insurgents had been fighting; and it was the shadow rather than the substance of independence with which France left the country.

Malta was another matter: Britain had agreed at Amiens to return the island to the Knights of St John, in spite of General Stuart's protests; but it was gradually being borne in on the minds of Addington and his colleagues that this would not do, and Charles' reports to Hobart can only have reinforced their doubts. Charles could tell them – if they did not already know – that France was busy widening her circle of influence in the Mediterranean; and they did not need to be told that if Malta were to be included in that circle, Britain would lose an important naval base. Nobody could suppose that either the Knights or the Tsar could be relied on to protect British interests; and, ironically, Charles' information was that the ordinary Maltese people would choose British rule if they were free to do so.[17]

While Charles was at Vienna, his younger brother, John, was serving in the Royal Navy in the Mediterranean. He was captain, in the rank of commander, of the sloop *Termagant*, which was used to carry instructions and dispatches, chiefly between Naples and Malta. The brothers communicated with each other through the British mission at Naples.[18] John was interested in whatever news Charles was free to give him, and he was able to give Charles information about foreign shipping and foreign ports; and soundings that he took in certain foreign ports proved valuable to the Admiralty when war broke out again.[19]

There is much in Charles' reports to Hobart on the subject of indemnities – that is, the compensation to be awarded to the German states for the transfer of the left bank of the Rhine to France. These indemnities were worked out by a body of representatives of the states concerned, with France and Russia as mediators and Napoleon as the final arbiter, but the task was no easy one. Passions ran high on all sides, but particularly in Austria, which stood to lose all her former glory. 'I again take up my pen', Charles wrote to Hobart, on 27 July 1802, 'to give you the little intelligence we have acquired here respecting the indemnities, which in all probability are about to create more disorder and confusion than the war which has just so happily terminated'.[20]

But the final settlement of the question, set out in an edict endorsed by Napoleon, the *Imperial Recess* of 25 February 1803, is not part of Charles' private and secret story. It was the diplomatic twists and turns, the intrigues and the bribery and corruption that led up to it, any item of which might have had implications for Britain, that interested him, at least as far as his reports were concerned. The bribery and corruption was striking: 'The money secretly received by the mediating powers who effect these changes surpasses all calculation', he told Hobart, in a report of 31 October 1802; '£200,000 sterling was the price of the Bavarian indemnities alone'.[21]

It was in 1801 or 1802 that Charles engaged as a servant a young man called William Wood, who was to remain with him for thirty years, and was to be used by him, as Captain Masseria was used by General Stuart, in 'work of a confidential nature'. According to Lady Louisa Stuart, Charles' aunt, Wood became 'footboy, groom, postillion [and] odd man' to Lady Stuart, Charles' mother, in 1801; and 'the next year having got into a scrape with the parish on account of a damsel ten years older than himself, he begged to go abroad with Charles ...'.[22] Lady Louisa was writing much later, and her memory of the year may have let her down: if Wood joined Charles when he went abroad, it was in 1801 and not 1802.

We know that Wood combined smuggling and spying with the more conventional duties of a gentleman's servant, and one historian has pointed out that smuggling was often a cover for spying at this time, with both British and French governments turning a blind eye to the practice because both profited by it.[23] But our knowledge of Wood is based on stories handed down in his family, a few letters and occasional references in other records. The same historian has noted that Charles was careful not to put on paper more that concerned his clandestine activities than was absolutely necessary,[24] and Wood had less reason than his master to offer hostages to fortune in the form of records.

In the Archives Nationales in Paris, there is a letter, with other papers, dated 19 Nivose, 12, in the Republican Calendar, or 8 January 1804, from the Prefect of the Department of La

Manche to the Grand Judge and Minister of Justice, in whose office then were combined what had been the separate Ministries of Police and Justice, concerning a group of men who claimed to be shipwrecked American sailors.[25] Unfortunately for these men, their stories did not tally. It was assumed that they were Englishmen, and they were made prisoners of war. One of them was a man whose name was given as William Woods [*sic*], aged 22, and it may be that he and Charles' servant were one and the same. The spelling of the prisoner's name is a minor point, and we know that Charles' servant was baptised on 26 December 1781,[26] so that he was roughly twenty-two years old at the time of the imprisonment of his nearly-namesake.

This story is the more interesting for the fact that it may link Wood and – through him – Charles with the great Cadoudal Plot, which failed. Georges Cadoudal was a leader of the Chouans, the Breton royalist insurgents, who proved his daring and his ruthlessness in an attempt to assassinate Napoleon in December 1800, and thereby commended himself to the more unscrupulous of the royalist *émigrés*. His own part in the plot was to kidnap Napoleon; a group of dissident army officers, led by Generals Pichegru and Moreau, was then to govern until the Louis XVIII returned from exile. The evidence is, however, that Napoleon would have been assassinated. The British government had a hand in the plot, but the lengths to which it would have gone in its collusion is a matter of speculation.[27]

Cadoudal crossed to France from England in August 1803, to meet fellow-conspirators in Paris. Napoleon and the French police had been made aware of what was afoot by their agents in London, however, and Cadoudal was arrested in March 1804. Other arrests took place in France, notably those of Pichegru and Moreau, and throughout Europe, wherever French writ ran. Already, in January 1804, according to one report, 'several suspects had been imprisoned in Normandy';[28]

we have no particular reason to believe that Wood was one of those suspects, but the coincidence of time and place suggests that their errands were not unconnected.

One of the French agents in London was a man called Mehée de la Touche, who penetrated the British Secret Service and was sent by Lord Hawkesbury on a probationary mission to Bavaria in September 1803. The British minister at Munich, Francis Drake by name, was suspicious of him but, following his own instructions from Hawkesbury, set him to rally the French *émigrés* in that part of Europe to the cause; and then, when the plot failed and many of those who had been involved in it were exposed, suffered for having done so.[29] The French government made the most of its propaganda coup, accusing Britain of planning to assassinate Napoleon, and Drake was one of those who had to be disowned.

In October 1803, Charles, as Chargé d'Affaires, was approached by a Frenchman whose name is not clear, with the offer of details of all confidential information passing between the French embassy in Vienna and the Ministry of Foreign Affairs in Paris, 'day by day as far as possible', and such additional information as he could obtain from other ministries.[30] He assured Charles that he had important contacts, and informed him that he had been sent to Vienna by the Grand Judge and Minister of Justice to report on all that concerned France there, privately and independently of the Ambassador.[31]

Shortly afterwards, Charles later reported, this man was returned to France unceremoniously: 'seized by desire of the French Ambassador and conveyed to the frontier under an escort of cavalry'.[32] Whatever his game had been he had not been able to play it out. He may simply have been a traitor to his country, but the explanation is unlikely to be as simple as that. There were various mutually inimical factions in the new French governing class, and intrigue was endemic at the highest levels; though that, in itself, is not an explanation. One

16

Napoleonic scholar has described the man as an *agent provocateur*, bent on discrediting Charles as Mehée had discredited Drake.[33]

If Charles' servant William Wood and the prisoner of the French, William Woods, were indeed one and the same, and if he was in Normandy at the end of 1803 or the beginning of 1804 on some errand for Charles to do with the Cadoudal Plot, loose ends remain. We do not know what his errand was, and we do not know how he escaped from the French and rejoined Charles. But the coincidences may be real: smugglers and spies, and others who did not wish to draw attention to themselves, frequently came and went between England and France through Normandy, often using the Channel Islands as staging posts.

Another member of Charles' household was engaged at about this time, according to Lady Louisa Stuart.[34] This was Alonzo or Alonso, almost always referred to simply in this way, but identified fully on one occasion, by Charles, as Mr J. Roman Alonso.[35] He is described variously in the records as valet, secretary and 'a foreign clerk and valet'.[36]

3

'The Secret Articles' 1804–1807

The first Napoleonic War broke out in 1803. Addington had been persuaded that it was impossible to live at peace with Napoleon and had refused to part with Malta, thus breaching the terms of the Treaty of Amiens and throwing down the gauntlet. William Pitt returned to power a year later, and at the same time Charles Stuart was appointed Secretary of Embassy at St Petersburg. Charles was instructed to stay at Vienna for the time being, however, and it was not until the end of October 1804 that he found himself again in the Russian capital. He sailed from England with the newly-appointed Ambassador, Lord Granville Leveson Gower.

Napoleon had been preparing to strike at England across the Channel, but the formation of the Third Coalition, of England, Russia and Austria, in August 1805, which threatened his flank, and Nelson's victory at Trafalgar in October, which left him without hope of controlling the Channel for a crossing, made him turn about. England was given a respite but not a reprieve. An Austrian army was defeated at Ulm, the day before Trafalgar, and a combined Austrian and Russian army was defeated at Austerlitz in December. Then, in January 1806, came the death of Pitt and the replacement of his administration by the 'Ministry of All the Talents'. And, later that year, Prussia entered the fray against Napoleon, but was promptly knocked out of it.

Charles was Minister Plenipotentiary *ad interim* at St Petersburg from July 1806, when Lord Granville was recalled at his own request, officially if not actually, until July 1807.[1] In March 1807 Charles went home on leave and in that same month the 'Ministry of All the Talents' collapsed, to be replaced by the Portland administration. The new Foreign Secretary, George Canning, was faced at once with a crisis in Britain's relationship with Russia, now under great pressure from Napoleon, but he was able to take advantage of a longstanding friendship with Lord Granville to persuade the reluctant Ambassador to return to his post, taking Charles with him. They left England again in May.

Lord Granville's instructions were to keep Tsar Alexander loyal to Britain at all costs, but it was too late: none of the arguments that the Ambassador could deploy had the force of Napoleon's army. What was left of the Russian and Prussian armies had retreated towards the Russian border; and it was at the border, at Tilsit, on the eve of Russia's last stand at Friedland, that Lord Granville was unfortunate enough to have to present himself. Friedland was a disaster, and Lord Granville and Charles, with other members of Alexander's entourage, were kept kicking their heels at the port of Memel, while Alexander, himself, prepared for his fateful meeting with Napoleon.

The story of Tilsit is well known: Napoleon and Alexander met on 25 June 1807, on a suitably fitted-up raft in the middle of the river Neimen, and were soon surprisingly *en rapport*; further meetings took place in the town during the next few days, and on 7 July a treaty was signed. It transpired that this treaty provided for the division of Europe between France and Russia, but there was much that did not transpire, and it was obvious to Canning that this was the case. Canning had his own information, however, and on the basis of this he warned his colleagues that Napoleon intended to annex neutral Denmark and turn her fleet against England. The implications were dire. No peaceful way out of the situation could be found, and the Foreign Secretary persuaded the Cabinet to sanction an attack on Copenhagen and the seizure of the Danish fleet.

The information on which Canning based his judgement came from a variety of sources. He had dispatches from diplomats in the field, such as Lord Granville at Memel, and reports from travellers abroad. Enclosed in one of Lord Granville's dispatches was a letter to him from Colin Mackenzie, described by one of Canning's biographers as 'a British soldier of fortune'[2] and by other historians as a British agent.[3] Mackenzie had made the most of an acquaintanceship with the Russian General Bennigsen at Tilsit, but the only significant inference to be drawn from his letter was that Alexander had changed sides.[4] Other agents, too, must have been at work.

Tradition has it that Canning's information consisted of the so-called secret articles of the Treaty of Tilsit. The tradition has been handed down in various forms, the most appealing of which is that it was Mackenzie who discovered what the secret articles were, by eavesdropping behind a curtain on the raft while the two Emperors hatched their plots.[5] Unfortunately, this does not square with Mackenzie's letter to Lord Granville or with what is known of his later movements.[6] The facts are that secret clauses existed; they could have confirmed Canning in his beliefs, but they did not see the light of day until much later.[7]

What is particularly interesting in the context of the story of Charles and his servant, William Wood, is that Canning received secret information from Tilsit during the night of 21 July,[8] and claimed that this justified the attack on Copenhagen.[9] He evidently did not care to admit that the decision to mount the attack was taken on or about 16 July.[10] His informant is not known: Mackenzie has been suggested,[11] but ruled out;[12] whoever it was has been said to have been a foreigner, on grounds that seem far from firm;[13] and there is a possibility that it was Wood, presumably acting for Charles or Lord Granville.

Wood's great-grandson, Guy Turner, committed some of the family's stories to paper in May 1934,[14] and a later member of the family elaborated on them in private conversations.[15] They are not reliable as history, but they may be based on fact. Another source is the reminiscences of one Henry Walter, who worked with men who themselves had worked for Wood in a nursery business that he founded.[16] According to Walter, Wood acted as a courier for Charles, sometimes disguised as a travelling salesman; and, according to the family, it was he who brought the secret articles to London.[17] We know that he cannot have delivered the secret articles, but perhaps he delivered Canning's secret information of the night of 21 July.

That there was need for subterfuge and cunning in the transmission of intelligence goes without saying, and the means used were naturally the means of the time. Particularly sensitive material was carried either by Foreign Service (King's) messengers or by special agents, and the latter might be personal servants, such as Wood and Alonzo. 'My dear Lord', Charles, as Minister *ad interim* a St Petersburg, wrote to Lord Granville, at home in England, one day in 1806, 'Although I have hardly a minute to addresss you before the departure of my servant . . .'.[18] Even in peacetime, a Foreign Service messenger's job was a dangerous one: 'There were many fatalities in the line of duty'.[19] And it can be assumed that the French and the Russians did their best to prevent the leakage of confidential information from Tilsit.

Diplomatic relations between Britain and Russia were not broken off at once, and Lord Granville and Charles followed the Tsar back to St Petersburg. Alexander was alarmed by the attack on Copenhagen and demanded an explanation. 'Self-preservation', Lord Granville is supposed to have replied, without wasting words.[20] In October, however, when Russia's ports were icebound again, and safe from attack, Alexander declared war. Lord Granville returned to England, with Charles.

But before he left Russia, Charles made secret arrangements to keep in touch with friends in the country. Our knowledge of these comes from a letter addressed to Canning by the Comte d'Antraigues, dated 13 April 1808.[21] It begins with a reference to 'the departure of Mr Stuart's valet' on an unspecified mission, and it is annotated 'Relative to Mr Stuart's secret mode of transmitting papers to Russia'. Alonzo is not mentioned by name in this letter, or, for that matter, in the letter from Charles to Lord Granville already quoted in this context, but correspondence of a later date confirms that he acted as a courier.[22]

The connection between Charles and the Comte d'Antraigues, whatever it may have been, is interesting: d'Antraigues was one of the best known of the French agents of the time. He was an ardent royalist, but had little respect for Louis XVIII or, indeed, for authority in any form, and one of his biographers has described him as 'pushy, arrogant, and ruthless'.[23] He depended on patronage, however, and at this time he was living in London and acting as an intermediary between Canning and contacts in Russia.[24] Chief among these contacts was Prince Czartoryski, who had been one of the Tsar's most influential advisers before Tilsit and was to regain his position in due course. D'Antraigues was assassinated four years later, on whose orders it is not known.

4

'A Special Service' 1808–1809

The year 1808 saw the beginning of the Peninsular War. France gave up all pretence that Spain was an ally rather than a puppet, replacing Ferdinand VII on the throne with Napoleon's brother, Joseph, and moved to take control of Britain's ancient ally, Portugal; but both Spain and Portugal proved difficult to subdue. Charles was in Madrid in May when the citizens rose against their oppressors,[1] and it soon became known that their example had been followed in many other parts of Spain.

This was good news for Britain, and Canning and the Minister for War in the Portland Administration, Lord Castlereagh, were determined to exploit Napoleon's discomfiture to the full. An important requirement was a reliable channel of communication between the Spanish patriots and the British government, but it would be no easy matter either to set up or to maintain such a channel. Since the rising in Madrid, Spain had become 'a conglomeration of city-states and autonomous provinces ruled by committees (juntas) of local notables',[2] each with its own problems and priorities, and there was no individual or body representative of them all.

Canning chose Charles for the job: he called it 'a special service' and in his instructions, dated 6 July,[3] he made it clear that, however it was presented, it was first and foremost an intelligence mission. Charles was to be based at Corunna:

From the inclosed [*sic*] copy of a letter which, by His Majesty's Command, I have written to the Galician Deputies, you will perceive that you are described as being charged with the carrying on of the communication between this country and Spain. In this character you will express your desire to receive from the Galician Government a communication of any military events or other occurrences of importance of which they may be able to obtain information.

And Canning returned to the subject of intelligence later in his instructions:

During your residence in Corunna, you will not rely solely on the Government of Galicia for information of events which may occur in the several provinces of Spain, but you will endeavour to procure a knowledge of them through every possible channel, and you will transmit to me by the packet-boats, which will shortly be established between Falmouth and Corunna, the most accurate intelligence which you may be able to obtain.

Since Britain was technically at war with Spain, and would remain so, it was assumed, until Spain was free again, Charles could not be given formal diplomatic status; he was not given much assistance either. The papers of his friend Charles Vaughan, scholar, traveller and future diplomat, show that, at first, his party consisted of himself and a servant, Vaughan and a servant and, also, a Mr Walpole.[4] Charles' servant is not named in any of his own or Vaughan's papers: he may have been William Wood and he may have been Alonzo. Walpole, referred to by Violet Stuart Wortley strangely as 'Honourable Walpole', but not identified,[5] acted as Charles' secretary, though he, like Vaughan, was with him as a friend.[6]

Charles wasted no time. He landed at Corunna on 20 July to

a warm – even tumultuous – welcome, and was presented to the junta of Galicia the next day, with General Sir Arthur Wellesley, the future Duke of Wellington, who was on his way to Portugal. His first dispatch to Canning is dated 22 July,[7] and it consists chiefly of a survey of the military and political situation in Spain, which was chaotic. In a covering letter,[8] he assured the Foreign Secretary that he was doing all he could to bring order out of the chaos. He had urged the junta to establish proper communications with all parts of the country not under French control, and to take whatever steps were necessary to set up a provisional central government.

He spent a month at Corunna, and the house in which he was lodged – the best in the town and known as *el palacio*, according to Vaughan[9] – became a clearing-house for intelligence – military, political and commercial. To it came couriers from Spanish juntas and generals, messengers from the British consuls newly re-established at opposite ends of the country, at Gijon and Cadiz, British officers and anonymous agents; and from it, to waiting packet-boats in the harbour, went his servant with dispatches for Canning. The Foreign Minister had made particular mention, in his instructions, of the consul at Gijon, John Hunter, also described as 'agent for British prisoners in Spain', as a source of information.[10]

The port of Ferrol, with its naval base and arsenal, attracted Charles' personal attention. Hedging his bets as to the course of the war, whatever the ostensible reason for his visit, he and a party of British officers, whom he had sensibly taken with him and seem to have been allowed to see all that there was to be seen,[11] collected a mass of information. His dispatch to Canning was followed by a letter, in which he referred to the visit again:

While at Ferrol I was anxious that the port should be properly and thoroughly examined by naval and military men. It is the fault of the officers who went with me if

27

they do not know that place at present as well as Portsmouth.[12]

After only a week, however, Charles had decided that Corunna was too far from the action, and had put it to Canning that he should move south.[13] Canning's response has been lost, but his decision may have been dictated by events. The provincial juntas agreed to a meeting of representatives, with a view to the formation of a single united junta and, after that, the setting up of a provisional central government. This meeting was to be held at Aranjuez, outside Madrid, as soon as the necessary arrangements could be made, and Charles was asked to be present, 'for the purpose' – he explained to Canning – 'of communicating their proceedings to His Majesty's Government'.[14]

A single united junta, the Central Junta, was duly formed, and its first meeting was held in the royal palace at Aranjuez on 25 September. To the dismay of many, including Charles, it then set itself up as the provisional central government, though it did not have popular support and – what was worse – it did not have the support of the Spanish generals. It was recognised as the provisional legitimate government of Spain by the British government, however, and Charles was superseded, as a consequence, by a properly accredited minister, John Hookham Frere. However, it was agreed that, instead of returning to England, Charles should stay where he was, in Spain, and assist Frere by liaising between the British generals in the peninsula and the Central Junta.[15]

A British army from Portugal, under General Sir John Moore, was to be joined by another from England, and this combined force, under General Moore, was to link up with a combined force of Spanish armies and sweep the French out of Spain. That was the plan. Unfortunately, Moore never had the full cooperation of his allies, and though the first part of the plan was successful the second was not. The Spanish generals, who had no effective commander-in-chief and could not agree among themselves, were outclassed when Napoleon took temporary command of the French forces in Spain. In the end, there was no Spanish army with which the British army could link up. The epic retreat to Corunna followed, and though what was left of the army was saved Moore, himself, was killed.

Charles enjoyed Moore's confidence from the first;[16,17] and, according to Vaughan, he was well liked by the Spanish,[18] who were particularly pleased by his grasp of their language.[19] In spite of Charles' liaison work, and in spite of the fact that British officers were attached to the staffs of the Spanish generals, however, the sort of information about the Spanish armies that might have prevented disaster was lacking. Moore unburdened himself to Charles on this subject in a letter on 10 November:[20]

> Our numerous correspondents with the various armies seem to have kept us in very complete ignorance of their state, either as to number or quality; had I been better informed I should have acted differently; as it is, I must take my chance and act for the best as circumstances arise.

But the retreat to Corunna was still some weeks away when Charles was involved in a small adventure of his own.[21] By the end of November 1808 the French were expected almost daily at the gates of Madrid, and during the night of 1 December Charles was warned that they were not far away. There was panic in the city, and for fear of treachery the inhabitants were forbidden to leave. This fear was by no means unjustified, but it merged into paranoia, and anyone who ignored it was likely to pay with his life. Charles coolly gathered the British residents at his house, and then, as the French approached, persuaded or inveigled an official into having the gates opened for him. It had been impossible to procure transport of any

29

sort, and the party walked twenty-eight miles to Aranjuez.

For the time being, the French were again masters of Spain. The Spanish armies had been defeated and the British Army driven out, and only the guerillas continued the fight. The Central Junta retired, first to Seville and then to Cadiz, where it disintegrated. But Charles had created a network of contacts that was to stand him and the British cause in good stead.

5

'Wellington's Right-hand Man'
1809–1814

During the first phase of the Peninsular War, in 1808, Charles was in the anomalous position of being the King's representative in Spain 'without a public diplomatic character',[1] diplomatic relations between Britain and Spain having been broken off in 1804. He spent most of the second phase of the war, from the beginning of 1810, in Portugal as His Majesty's duly accredited Minister at Lisbon, but anomaly dogged him: the Prince Regent of Portugal had escaped to Brazil at the beginning of the war, leaving behind him a Regency Council, and Charles was made a member of that Council so that, for as long as he was in Portugal, he was both the British minister and one of the governors of the kingdom. What was more important to both Britain and Portugal, if not to the whole of Europe, however, was that he was 'Wellington's right-hand man'.[2]

At the stage of the war at which Charles arrived in Portugal, the country had twice been overrun by the French, and the Regency Council and the Prince Regent, himself, were urging attack as the best form of defence against a third invasion. Wellington, who was Commander-in-Chief of the British Army in Portugal and the Portuguese Army, knew better, and that did not make him popular in Lisbon or Rio de Janeiro. His forces were not strong enough for a campaign against the

31

French in Spain – which is what an offensive strategy would have meant – without the full support of the Spanish Army, and recent experience had taught him that he could not rely on the cooperation of the Spanish generals. Indeed, the Spanish generals could not be relied on to cooperate with each other.

By that stage of the war, too, a military intelligence organisation had evolved in Portugal and Spain. Colonel Sir George Murray, Wellington's Quartermaster-General, who had previously been in charge of the Plans branch of the Depot of Military Knowledge, formed a Corps of Guides, largely of Portuguese and Spanish partisans and French deserters with a knowledge of both language and terrain.[3] Wellington was impressed by this Corps, not only as a body of guides but also as a group from which could be drawn interrogators, couriers and special agents, and he had it made officially part of his army.[4] Thereafter, the ordinary services of guides were obtained from local people, when and where necessary.

In effect, this intelligence organisation had three sections: infantry scouts and cavalry patrols carried out reconnaissance; a changing team of local people provided interpreters and guides; and the Corps of Guides, with British officers and men on its strength, had duties that included the collection of information from behind the enemy's lines. The best-known of the officers of the Corps were Colquhoun Grant, Charles Somers Cocks, Andrew Leith Hay and John Waters, but there were many others. None of them liked to think of himself as a spy, though they were all, in fact, engaged in espionage, and Grant was eventually captured by the French because he insisted on wearing full uniform, with a scarlet tunic.[5]

Much use was made by these men of contacts in French-held territory and among guerrilla bands. Clergy were often particularly helpful, since they could come and go more or less freely without being challenged. Guerrillas could be relied on to have paid attention to French troop movements and they were often found to have possessed themselves of important information about both the tactics and the strategy of the enemy, by the simple expedient of abducting couriers. Elizabeth Longford noted that 'furious partisan war against Napoleon's couriers helped to perfect Wellington's intelligence system'.[6] Lady Longford also remarked, however, that Wellington's men had great difficulty in breaking French codes.[7]

There were undoubtedly many other sources of information. In a paper entitled 'Espionage in Time of Peace', prepared for the Army General Staff in January 1909, there is an interesting reference to Wellington and the Peninsular War:[8]

> Wellington in the Peninsular War was always well provided with intelligence which was obtained for him by the local authorities. They employed as agents itinerant musicians including a guitar player of considerable repute, beggars, smugglers etc. One of the most useful was a cobbler, who had a shop at the end of the bridge of Irun, where, always plying his trade he counted every French soldier who entered or left Spain by that route and transmitted the news to Lisbon by coasting vessels.

The cobbler was well placed: Irun was on the French troops' route into Spain from their base at Bayonne.

Wellington was sometimes involved in high political intrigue, for which he had no taste. In 1809, for instance, when he was still Sir Arthur Wellesley, a French officer called Argenton, from Marshal Soult's army at Oporto, was brought to see him at Lisbon, with a story of conspiracy against both Soult and Napoleon. According to Argenton, Soult was to be ousted and his army was to be marched back to Paris to overthrow Napoleon. He asked for passports for himself and other officers, to enable them to return to France by sea and prepare for the coup. Castlereagh, still Minister for War, when consulted, suspected that an attempt was being made to mislead Britain in some way, though he was sufficiently aware

33

of the state of affairs in France not to discount the story completely, and the passports were not forthcoming.[9]

There was a third invasion of Portugal by the French, in the autumn of 1810, but though Wellington had been unable to prevent it he had prepared for it, with a scorched earth policy and lines of defence across the country at Torres Vedras. The French were brought to a halt at the lines of Torres Vedras, and then forced to withdraw due to winter weather and lack of food and forage. But the blame for the sufferings of the Portuguese people outside the lines, left to the mercies of the French and themselves affected by the scorched earth policy, was laid at Wellington's door. Wellington had gained time to build up his forces, however, and in the early summer of 1811 he drove the French out of Portugal once and for all. For the duration of the Peninsular War, and for as long as Charles remained in Portugal, the action was in Spain.

Charles' task was particularly difficult in the first two years of his appointment. He was looking after British interests in a country that a British general had been brought in to defend and had allowed to be laid waste; and, at the same time, he was in a position of responsibility and trust in the government of that country: conflicts of interest were always likely to occur or, at least, always likely to be suspected. There was continual criticism of Charles and Wellington and much intrigue against them as well. Soon after his arrival, Charles had to deal with a devious attempt to have Wellington's defensive strategy overruled by the British government, and the General wrote to him: 'It appears that you have had a sharp contest with the [Portuguese] Government respecting our plan of operations. They will end by forcing me to quit them, and then they will see how they will get on'.[10]

Charles' headquarters was his house, and there are references to this and his style of life in various records, including some of his own surviving letters. He told his mother that it was a fine house and, having emphasised the point that he was working hard, went on to tell her that his dining table was always crowded and that he gave a ball or a concert every fortnight.[11] Officers of the two services were welcome at any time, without invitation, and he must have found their company interesting. Whether or not any of the officers of the Corps of Guides came to the house we do not know, but Charles Somers Cocks' younger brother, James, certainly did.[12]

Sir Thomas Graham, later Lord Lynedoch, Wellington's second-in-command, said it was a beautiful house set in a beautiful garden outside the city.[13] Samuel Broughton, the army surgeon, talked of 'dancing and cards, in addition to occasional dinner-parties and more select evening assemblies'.[14] One of Charles' friends teased him with affairs of the heart,[15] and it is true that there was at least one lady, a certain Condessa d'Amadia, with whom his relationship became close. He and the Condessa are said to have corresponded over many years, though their letters have not survived, and she is said to have brought him much useful information, particularly concerning relationships between Lisbon and Rio de Janeiro.[16]

Contact between Charles and Wellington was as close as the war allowed. All Wellington's dispatches to Castlereagh and his successors as Minister of War were sent to Charles for his perusal before they were sent on,[17] and the dispatches were supplemented by private letters, of which there was a constant stream. Charles was also sent résumés of all the intelligence obtained by Marshal Beresford, of the Portuguese Army.[18] From Charles to Wellington passed instructions from London, information from the Regency Council at Lisbon and the Prince Regent at Rio de Janeiro, and items of intelligence from a variety of sources. Some of these sources were responsible to Wellington and used the British Mission to find him, but others were responsible to Charles himself.

There are several references in the records to information with which Charles was able to provide Wellington. With one letter, on 8 April 1811, he enclosed a report from 'an agent in Bayonne',[19] which has not been found, and in a second letter, on 17 May 1811, he said 'another person in my employment has just arrived here from Bayonne'; and he added a full note of what he had learned from this person. Perhaps he compared it with information received from the cobbler of Irun:

His report respecting the passage of troops tallies with former events. I think it right however to send you details from 1st January till 22nd April, the statement of passage of prisoners into France and the persons he met on his way to the frontier.[20]

In February 1811, just before the French withdrew from the lines of Torres Vedras, Charles took part in a counter-espionage operation mounted by Wellington.[21] A certain General Pamplona, at the French headquarters at Torres Novas, had set up a spy network through which the enemy was obtaining information from Lisbon, and Charles was asked to track down his contacts in the capital. Meanwhile, Wellington suggested to Beresford that he should arrange for raiding parties to visit the known collaborators linked to the network in French-occupied Portugal, and either seize them and their papers or persuade them to work for him.[22] Colquhoun Grant was to take part in the operation at this stage.[23]

Wellington explained to Charles how the information was being transmitted:

This correspondence has been carried out principally through the means of persons who go into the enemy's lines with coffee, sugar, etc., to sell, which goods they dispose of at large prices; and they generally carry a letter either to or fro. Then there are others employed purposely to carry on the correspondence, who are inhabitants of Torres Vedras; but these have been so badly paid, and so ill treated, that they do not do the business with great alacrity, or with much regularity, and they seldom return the second time.[24]

Nothing is known of Charles' part in the operation, but there would have been no shortage of suspects for him to investigate. He would have been able to start with the French spies and *agents provocateurs* already under surveillance in Lisbon, and he would have assumed that there were others. He would also have been interested in possible collaborators among the Portuguese inhabitants of the city, including members of the Portuguese aristocracy. There were many among the aristocracy whose pride was deeply hurt by Britain's temporary ascendancy in their country: Charles was a member of the Regency Council and Wellington was Commander-in-Chief of the Allied Army; and, if that was not enough, Marshal Beresford was an Irishman. One conspiracy at this time is known to have been dealt with rigorously by the Portuguese authorities.[25]

There are other references to spies and intelligence officers disguising themselves as pedlars, or doubling as such, in the accounts of the Peninsular War. Charles Somers Cocks' servant wrote to a friend, from Lisbon on 14 February 1810, to say that he had just been reunited with his master after the latest of the latter's adventures:

The dragoon that was with the Captain tells me that when the Captain was ill of a fever after the Battle of Talavera he was so weak for sometime that the man was obliged to carry him about on his back, but he has the character of having done more for the service in the time than any officer in the army. He has been more than once selling gin, etc. amongst the French lines, but I have not had time to get any particulars, as we are so busy preparing for our departure.[26]

37

Such accounts give credibility to some of the stories told about William Wood. One of them comes from Henry Walter: 'He used to tell his workmen he followed both the Allied Army and the French armies as well, as a trader in hardware goods, and traded news as well to each'.[27] Another comes from Guy Turner, who believed that the setting for it was the Waterloo campaign, though the Peninsular War seems more likely:

> At that time my Great-grandfather three times went through the French lines as a spy. Once, when selling ribbons and trinkets to the soldiers, he was suspected and taken before a tribunal to be searched. Climbing on to the table, he threw down his cap, saying: 'Search me; I've nothing to conceal.' They cut his clothes to ribbons, tore off the buttons and linings - in fact, left him naked; and finding nothing, brought him more clothes. He dressed, picked up his cap and walked out – with despatches for the Duke of Wellington sewn underneath the button of his cap.[28]

There is no doubt that Charles Stuart had his own intelligence organisation in the Peninsula, and the speed with which it was activated when he arrived in Portugal suggests that he was able to make use of contacts that he had already made in Spain. It is rare to find a direct reference to it in the records, but there is one in a letter from Wellington to Charles of 21 April 1810. Wellington's Corps of Guides had yet to show its full potential:

> It would be very desirable to establish the channel of communication which you propose, and I strongly recommend you to establish it. We are sadly deficient in good information, and all the efforts which I have made to obtain it have failed; and all that we know is the

movement of the troops at the moment, or probably after it is made.[29]

Charles' intelligence interests went beyond the Peninsula, too. He used to send summaries of his dispatches for Castlereagh to Lord William Bentinck, British Minister at Palermo and British Commander-in-Chief in the Mediterranean, who was planning a diversionary landing on the Mediterranean coast of Spain.[30] With one of these summaries, on 10 March 1813, Charles enclosed a letter addressed to a certain Mme Calvet, and a covering note to Bentinck:

> I shall be obliged to you to transmit the enclosed letter to its address, obtaining a receipt that it has been delivered and sending me either the answer or any other letter which Mme Calvet may be desirous to send to Portugal.[31]

This is the language of business rather than pleasure.

The battle lines moved steadily eastward, and on 11 July 1813, Charles told Castlereagh, now Foreign Secretary, that he was too far from 'the theatre of war' to be able any longer to keep him in touch with it.[32] Meanwhile, Britain's allies in the Fourth Coalition were pushing westward from the other end of Europe. Paris fell on 31 March 1814, and Napoleon abdicated on 6 April.

6

The First Restoration and The Second Napoleonic War 1814–1815

Charles' star was in the ascendant at the First Restoration of the Bourbons in 1814. His services in the Peninsula had been rewarded with a knighthood in 1812, and his diplomatic qualifications had been recognised by appointments, first, as Minister *ad interim* at Paris in the summer of 1814 and, secondly, as Ambassador at the Hague from the beginning of 1815. He was made a Privy Councillor at home in England in 1814, between these two appointments.[1]

Only a matter of weeks separated Charles' arrival in the Netherlands and Napoleon's escape from Elba. Louis XVIII fled ignominiously from Paris, to Ghent in Belgium, and the Hundred Days began. Belgium had been to all intents and purposes a part of France since the Revolutionary War, but Britain and her allies in the war that had just ended, following up their victory, had transferred its territory to Holland, to form the Kingdom of the Netherlands. Their intention had been to buttress Holland against any future threat from France and, at the same time, to remove the potential threat posed to other countries, Britain in particular, by France's control of Antwerp and the Scheldt. It was likely that the recovery of Belgium would be one of Napoleon's first objectives.

The Duke of Wellington was appointed Commander-in-Chief of the British and Dutch-Belgian forces in the Netherlands, with his headquarters at Brussels, and Charles was again at his service. This was a matter of satisfaction to both of them, according to Charles, who told Lady Elizabeth Yorke, his future wife, that though he would like to be in England, with her, he was proud of the fact that the Duke would not give up his claims on him.[2] Perhaps Charles' most important contribution to the Waterloo campaign was to keep in check French influence on the civil administration of the Netherlands. Belgium had been French for so long that the loyalties of many officials, and many of the population at large, lay more naturally with Napoleon than with their new King.

Charles was now also appointed Ambassador at the court of Louis XVIII in exile. There, espionage and intrigue were part of everyday life. Napoleon and Napoleon's Minister of Police, Fouché, both had spies at Ghent. Fouché had lost faith in Napoleon, but he was a regicide – he had voted for the death of Louis XVI – and he could expect no favours from the Bourbons, unless he could make himself as useful to them as he had been to revolutionaries and usurpers. Talleyrand, Foreign Minister to Napoleon in his heyday and then to Louis XVIII during the First Restoration, who led a charmed life as one regime followed another, was also waiting and watching and working out his next move. He had represented France at the Congress of Vienna, convened to settle the affairs of Europe so comprehensively unsettled by Napoleon, and he had wisely decided to prolong his stay in Austria.

Then there were those who would have liked to see Louis XVIII's brother, the Comte d'Artois, or his cousin, Louis Philippe, Duc d'Orléans, on the throne. Artois, at Ghent, personified the most extreme and uncompromising royalist opinion, and he had considerable influence on the King. His support was limited, however, and came chiefly from French émigrés. Louis Philippe was in England, holding himself aloof from the proceedings at Ghent and discreetly advertising his liberal credentials. The Tsar was one of his most powerful supporters, and Fouché and Talleyrand thought it worth their while to cultivate him. When the King suggested that he should come to Ghent, where his activities could more easily be monitored, he declined to do so, and Charles was employed to pour oil on troubled waters.[3]

Spies, intrigants and others would have liked to know whom the British government wished to see on the throne, since the opportunity for a fresh choice was likely soon to present itself. The government did not intend to commit itself at this stage, since it could not please all its friends and allies and did not wish to offend any of them, but Castlereagh was of the opinion that it would not be right or expedient to withdraw support from Louis XVIII. The Prime Minister, Lord Liverpool agreed with him, and so did Wellington. Castlereagh was not blind to the King's faults, however, and he was aware of the fact that the worst of them derived from His Most Christian Majesty's belief in his Divine Right.

For political reasons, therefore, British policy had to be presented, for the time being, as anti-Napoleon but not pro-Bourbon. Castlereagh decided to make use of whatever time there was to groom the King for a Second Restoration, with instruction in the theory and practice of constitutional monarchy. It was an extraordinary undertaking and Castlereagh entrusted it to Charles, whose ordinary diplomatic duties gave him cover.[4] But it could not be left entirely to Charles, and Castlereagh supervised his efforts in a private correspondence, part of the interest of which lies in what it reveals of the Foreign Secretary's thinking:

> So far from making himself visibly responsible for everything, the King ought to throw upon his Ministers the odium and risk of conducting his service. His Majesty ought to turn the political control towards the Minister for the time being and not entertain it himself beyond affording him the due support which his services may

deserve. This is the true strength of a constitutional king.[5]

He went on, in the same letter, perhaps cynically:

All paper constitutions are of comparatively small importance; the essence of a free state is so to manage the party warfare, as to reconcile it with the safety of the sovereign – to do this, the King must give the contending parties facilities against each other, and not embark himself too deeply with any.

When Napoleon marched into Belgium and fighting began, Charles was instructed to make the safety of Louis XVIII his first concern. Wellington thought Napoleon's most likely approach to Brussels would be clockwise, to cut him off from the sea and, incidentally, to pick up the King as a prize on his way, but he did not wish to make his final dispositions until he could be sure that Napoleon would not take the most direct route from Paris, through Mons. In spite of the threat to the King at Ghent, Charles preferred to be in Brussels during those fateful days of 1815; and he was at the Duchess of Richmond's Ball, on 15 June, when Wellington was brought the news that the French army was moving rapidly in an anticlockwise direction towards Charleroi.

Wellington had been caught out, but this was due to bad luck rather than bad management on his part. For the first time, a British army in the field had an intelligence department, and this was headed by Colquoun Grant, who had proved himself as an intelligence officer in the Peninsula.[6] Grant had contacts in Paris and agents along the border between France and Belgium, and it would have been difficult to fault his organisation. As soon as Napoleon's line of advance became clear to him, he sent a courier to Wellington with the information. The courier was intercepted by a cavalry patrol and taken to the hapless Hanoverian General Dörnberg, who judged his information worthless and sent him back to Grant.[7]

'It has been a damned nice thing – the nearest run thing you ever saw in your life',[8] Wellington told Creevey, several times over, soon after the Battle of Waterloo on 18 June. Wellington would have been better prepared if Grant's courier had got through to him; he would have been less sure of final victory, on the other hand, if the Prussian Marshal Blücher had not come to his assistance when he did or, alternatively, if the French Marshal Grouchy had either delayed Blücher for longer than he did or gone to Napoleon's assistance. Grouchy's conduct that day was used by Napoleon to explain, if not to excuse, his defeat, and it has been the subject of speculation since. What makes the episode relevant to Charles' story is that William Wood is said to have been involved in it.

Grouchy had command of the right wing of Napoleon's army, and his orders on 17 June were to pursue the Prussian army, which had been defeated at Ligny and was retreating eastward or north-eastward, as far as was known, and to prevent Blücher from joining forces with Wellington. When the noise of battle reached him and his men from Waterloo the next day, he was urged by General Gérard to turn back, but he refused to disobey his orders as he understood them. He had received several sets of orders during 17 and 18 June, and none of them was clear or unambiguous; but that did not save him from censure: he should have gone to Napoleon's assistance, and he did not do so. The opinion of military historians is that he simply lacked the qualities usually found in a commander of his rank and experience;[9] legend has it, however, that he was bribed.

According to this legend, Nathan Rothschild bribed Grouchy, and then leaked a false account of the transaction to cause a panic in the money markets, from which he could profit.[10] And according to Guy Turner, William Wood was the go-between:

Possibly the history of England might have been different had not my great-grandfather, as agent of the Secret Service, got to Marshal Grouchy before the Battle of Waterloo with a box containing 20,000 golden sovereigns. The intention, as you may know, was for Marshal Grouchy to join Napoleon and fight the British before Blücher could arrive with his army. Well! Old Mr Wood got there first with his bribe, in consequence of which the Marshal avowed the roads were too bad for him to join Napoleon, and as you all know, the armies under the Duke of Wellington [prevailed] at Waterloo. We still have in the family the identical brass bound box in which the money was taken to the Marshal.[11]

The discrepancies between the two stories may not be important, in the circumstances.

Napoleon made way for Louis XVIII, again; and, for the sake of expediency, Louis was persuaded to make Fouché and Talleyrand his ministers. Charles returned to Paris with the King and was eventually confirmed in office as Ambassador.

7

The Second Restoration 1815–1819

Duff Cooper set the scene in his biography of Talleyrand:

> The astonishing ease with which Napoleon effected the overthrow of the first Restoration made many tremble for the security of the second. It was a cloak and dagger period. Some of Balzac's stories which describe it are apt to strike the modern reader as too sensational. But he was writing of what he had seen. Dark conspiracies, secret societies, midnight meetings of desperate men, impossible plots – these were the order of the day; and real as a great deal of the danger may have been, it was many times exaggerated in the imaginations of the fearful.[1]

There were three major political groupings in France in the early years of the Restoration: the ultraroyalists, the royalists and the liberals. The ultraroyalists, who looked to the Comte d'Artois for leadership, were more royalist than the King, and some would have liked to see a counter-revolution. The royalists were those who believed in constitutional monarchy, and supported the version of it on offer. The liberals, or the left, made up a particularly heterogeneous grouping, which included Jacobins and revolutionaries but also left-wing pragmatists, some of them Bonapartists who preferred constitutional monarchy to autocracy. The ultraroyalists controlled parliament in 1815 and 1816, but in 1817, 1818 and 1819 a political balance was held by the royalists.

Within these groupings and other organisations, and separately and in their own right, too, there existed an unknown number of revolutionary cells, each with its own particular agenda. Some were linked on a regional or national basis, though the day of the national and international secret revolutionary societies that threatened the status quo in Germany, Spain, Italy and France was yet to come. Most conspiracies came to nothing, but there were episodes of violence both in Paris and in the country. There was a serious uprising at Grenoble in 1816, when a republican lawyer called Rey attempted to seize the town with a force made up largely of Napoleonic veterans. This was put down with a severity that was intended to be a deterrent to others, but may only have acted as a spur.[2]

Britain could not but be interested in political affairs in France, overt or covert, and the relationship between the two countries was an uneasy one. Britain's declared intention was to work for a peaceful and peaceable France, but there were those who suspected that her real policy was to foster political unrest in order to justify the continued occupation of the country. Wellington was the Commander-in-chief of the Army of Occupation, and he was also, for some time, in fact if not in theory, the chief representative of Britain in France. Hence, he was the focus of much resentment. Castlereagh was in Paris while the new peace treaty, the Second Treaty of Paris, was being negotiated, and he was as unpopular there as Wellington.

In this state of affairs, what had become known as 'His Majesty's Foreign Secret Service'[3] assumed greater importance than usual, and intelligence and counter-intelligence achieved a greater currency than usual. Castlereagh took a particular interest in the Secret Service and, in response to a letter on the subject from Charles to William Hamilton, one of his under-secretaries, to which Hamilton responded with the suggestion that more discretion and less naming of names would be advisable,[4] he gave his views on certain agents, at length and with names named. He took the precaution, however, of writing the letter himself at his own home and marking it 'Private and Secret'.[5]

One of the stories told about Castlereagh (who became Marquis of Londonderry in 1821) is that he left a cache of intercepted letters behind when he stayed at the Paris embassy in 1818.[6] They were not found until six years later, when Charles sent them to the Foreign Secretary of the time, Canning, with a covering note:

> The accompanying packet of papers were found two days since concealed in a sofa which was placed in the apartment occupied by the late Lord Londonderry during his visit to Paris shortly after the Congress of Aix-la-Chapelle. As they appear to be intercepted letters from foreign courts, I think it my duty to send them to you, taking care that no copies are left in the papers of the Embassy.[7]

Charles had not been in Paris more than three weeks when one of the many English visitors to the capital, Lady Granville, observed of him: 'He discovers what others are about or would be about to a degree that must be very useful to him in his present situation'.[8] He had not wasted any time, and one reason was that he felt some responsibility for the safety of Wellington and Castlereagh – which was the heavier for the fact that neither man was over-concerned for himself. There were at least two attempts on Wellington's life during this period,[9] and others may have been prevented by Charles' vigilance. A conspiracy against Castlereagh fizzled out.[10]

Charles could often work more or less confidently with the French authorities, but he could never assume their full and disinterested cooperation, any more than they could assume his. Nobody was punished for either of the best-known attempts on Wellington's life. The man who shot at him in one of these incidents, an old soldier, devoted to Napoleon, was tracked down and arrested, but was not convicted, in spite of the fact that there was never any doubt of his guilt. The court held that the evidence was not strong enough, but Charles suspected a political motive.[11] One of his agents attended the trial and took notes, which were sent to Castlereagh,[12] and, whether or not on the Foreign Secretary's instructions, he lodged an official complaint.[13]

This agent was one of several employed by Charles, and he was probably a man called Darby, who provided him with a weekly series of reports, neatly written in French. When Darby returned to England, Charles recommended him to Canning in a letter in which he also described his work:

> You are probably aware that during the last 8 years Mr Darby has been habitually employed by this Embassy for the purpose of collecting information, reporting the proceedings in the Chambers and in the Courts of Justice and communicating with journalists ...[14]

The Chambers were the Chamber of Deputies and the Chamber of Peers – the French Parliament.

Other agents obtained for Charles more confidential and politically sensitive material. In 1817, a change was made in the ministry presided over by the Duc de Richelieu and, with a dispatch dated 14 July 1817, Charles sent Castlereagh fourteen A5 sheets of closely written and now scarcely legible English, undated and unsigned. The contents, Charles explained to the Foreign Secretary, comprised 'a statement of the circumstances which led to the late change in the French ministry and upon which I have reason to believe your Lordship may rely'.[15]

But they could not always rely on their agents: indeed, they could be badly caught out. Castlereagh warned Charles against

50

a certain Mr Marshall, also known as Dr Griffith, with whom he was evidently having dealings.[16] Marshall was 'not only a great rogue in the ordinary sense of intrigue', said Castlereagh, 'but a very dangerous man'. He had played on Prussia's resentment of the leniency with which France had been treated after the Hundred Days, for example, and claimed to be the agent of a party planning the overthrow of Louis XVIII and his dynasty. The worst of it was, Castlereagh added, that he had led the Prussians to believe that Wellington and Richelieu were with them. The Foreign Secretary hoped Charles would agree that he was 'a two-edged tool', to be handled with care.

Informers may have offered better value for money than agents, but they, too, and their wares, had to be treated with caution. For some time, Charles was provided with what he was told were reports prepared by the Minister of Police, Louis XVIII's favourite, Decazes, for the King; and in one period of twelve months – April 1817 to April 1818 – there were between ninety and a hundred of these.[17] Then, early in 1819, by which time Richelieu had resigned, leaving his office to a figurehead while his power and influence passed to Decazes, now both Minister of Police and Minister of the Interior, Charles was informed by Hamilton that he was being duped. The Foreign Office had information that Decazes was feeding him the reports.[18]

As if to illustrate the point that nothing in the field of intelligence and counter-intelligence can be assumed to be what it seems to be, however, the story has an unexpected twist. It transpired that the reports were, indeed, intended for Charles by Decazes, who sent them to the informer via one of his secretaries in disguise. But it did not follow, Charles maintained, that they were bogus. And Hamilton agreed with him: 'I do not think they bear this character on the face of them', he said, 'tho' it is just possible at any rate'. 'However', the under-secretary concluded, having consulted Castlereagh, 'they are well worth their price and will of course be continued'.[19]

It is a strange story, but it is given added credibility by a published extract from French Secret Police records, concerning a remarkably similar situation:

> One can be certain that the reports that the various ministers make to His Majesty are immediately passed on to the British Ambassador. A certain baroness, who is very close to the King, delivers copies of all these reports, even the most secret, to an Englishman who has been living in France for some time. This individual passes them directly to His Excellency. He receives £40 sterling a month, which he shares with the person from whom he obtains the reports.[20]

And what is known about Decazes makes Machievellian behaviour seem the norm:

> From 1815 to 1818 Decazes was Minister of Police at a time when the police was unbelievably complex and very important: Balzac's secret societies, *contre-polices*, and crooks turned policemen, are no exaggeration. Perhaps it was inevitable that Decazes should display some of the characteristics of politicians who rely too much on secret information, *agents provocateurs* and intercepted letters. Metternich's love letters to Princess Lieven, Metternich's letters from Talleyrand, offering to sell him French official documents, and the Prussian Ambassador's despatches to Berlin, are only some of the correspondence intercepted by Decazes's agents and, at least in extracts, shown to Louis.[21]

Some of Charles' counter-espionage measures are referred to in his papers. An accusation in British newspapers of negligence in the handling of official documents between Paris and London caused him to describe his part in the procedure in a letter to Joseph Planta, Hamilton's fellow under-secretary. He dispatched a messenger to London every evening at six o'clock; important papers were never entrusted to any servant until they were placed in the bag, and they were not placed in the bag more than a few minutes before six o'clock.[22] The locks fitted to the doors of the embassy were specially made.[23] Cyphers were changed immediately if there was any suggestion that they had been compromised.[24]

More about Charles' security arrangements can be gathered from the records of the French Secret Police, who admitted that it was difficult to obtain information from the British embassy.[25] Charles kept all important papers in his own office, to which no servant was allowed access except under supervision, and those papers that were intended for London were dispatched on a daily basis. All locks had extra safety mechanisms – 'combinations devices, using figures and letters' – and only Charles and two of his staff held keys. As far as documents were concerned, according to the French agents, those that were interesting were not accessible and those that were accessible were not interesting.

But the Secret Police claimed to have certain of Charles' servants in their pay, and one of these servants was Alonzo.[26] He had been with Charles for ten years and was to remain with him for another ten, to part company with him finally on good terms.[27] He was also thought sufficiently trustworthy to be lent to Castlereagh while the Foreign Secretary was in Paris.[28] Perhaps he was not the loyal servant that Charles took him to be; perhaps, on the other hand, he double-crossed the French Secret Police. There is some indication that he manipulated the French agents. 'The operatives in charge', runs a note in their records, 'have had described to them in detail, by Master Alonzo, the circumstances that make it so difficult to obtain items of interest'.[29]

William Wood's name does not appear in the available records of the time in the context of espionage, but nothing can be inferred reliably from that. There is a suggestion that Charles used him as a special messenger, sending him instead of one of his usual messengers to London or Calais, for instance, when some particularly sensitive or otherwise important piece of information was to be transmitted,[30] but nothing more.

Another special messenger, of a different stamp, was Lord Lowther, Charles' cousin and one of a raffish group of his friends who were also members of the Prince Regent's circle. He and Charles shared an interest in the theatre and the opera, drawn as much by the artistes as by their art, we are told. But in Paris he mixed business with pleasure, acting as agent for the Prince Regent and carrying messages from Charles to Castlereagh.[31,32] It was part of Decazes' inscrutable behaviour that he cultivated Lowther: 'De Cazes [sic] writes me long political "statesman" letters', he wrote to Charles one day in 1816. 'What his object is I know not'.[33] He could only suppose – as the correspondence continued – that his object was to establish a channel of communication with the Prince Regent.[34]

Charles' secret activities on behalf of the Foreign Office were funded through an account opened for the purpose with Coutts & Co. This was known as his 'Separate Account', to distinguish it from his private account with the bank.[35] Money was paid into the Separate Account in London, usually by one of the Foreign Office clerks, and transferred to an account at Bagenault's Bank in Paris, from which Charles was able to pay his agents and informers.[36] Similar arrangements had been made since 1795, when Lord Grenville, the Foreign Secretary, sent William Wickham, his spymaster, to Switzerland to investigate a mysterious peace overture: 'When Wickham announced that he needed £3,000 at his disposal, Grenville opened a "Separate Account" with Coutts into which this sum was placed'.[37]

On two occasions in 1817 and another in 1818, relatively large sums were paid from Charles' Separate Account direct to Quentin Craufurd, a stout-hearted old gentleman whose involvement with Charles in this way is unsurprising. Craufurd made a fortune with the East India Company and settled in Paris, where he devoted himself to cultural pursuits. He was caught up in the maelstrom of the Revolution when he lent his support, in the form of cash and contacts, to the men who plotted to rescue the royal family, and he was personally involved, with Count Fersen, in the abortive flight to Varennes.[38] He thought it wise to leave France temporarily, but he returned to Paris at the Peace of Amiens. He was able to stay there when war broke out again, because – it is said – he enjoyed the friendship of Talleyrand.[39]

During his absence from France, Craufurd made himself useful to Grenville and Wickham, not least but not only by obtaining information for them from his contacts in Paris.[40] He had other sources of information, among them his nephews: James and George Craufurd were bankers at Rotterdam, and they, like the Rothschilds and other bankers, were sensitive to the least hint of change in the affairs of Europe;[41] Charles Gregan and Robert Craufurd were army officers, Charles with an appointment that allowed him to travel about Europe and Robert with no such appointment but some excuse to do likewise.[42] At one time, we are told, most of Britain's military intelligence from the Continent was supplied by Quentin, Charles Gregan and Robert Craufurd.[43]

Having returned to Paris, Craufurd spent the rest of his life in France, a period that included the Napoleonic Wars, the First Restoration and the early years of the Second Restoration. It would be difficult to believe that he had nothing more to do with intelligence work in all these eventful years, even without the evidence of the payments to him from Charles' Separate Account. Notes from Charles to Sir William a'Court, British Minister at Naples, enclosing letters from Craufurd to an unnamed correspondent, and requesting that precautions should be taken to see that the addressee and only the addressee should open them, can be taken as extra evidence,

55

circumstantial though it may be, that he did not confine himself to his cultural pursuits.[44]

When Craufurd died, in 1819, Charles bought from his estate a seventeenth-century copy of a Raphael portrait, *Giovanna of Aragon*. This now belongs to the Victoria and Albert Museum.[45]

Lord Stuart de Rothesay by Baron Gérard.

General Sir Charles Stuart as Lt. Col. of the 26th Regiment by George Romney.
Courtesy Glasgow City Council (Museums).

George Canning by Sir Thomas Lawrence (1825).
Courtesy of National Portrait Gallery, London.

The Duke of Wellington by Baron Gérard (circa 1814). This hangs in the British Embassy, Paris.
© Queen's Printer and Controller of HMSO, 2005.
Courtesy UK Government Art Collection.

Lord Castlereagh by Sir Thomas Lawrence (1809-1810).
Courtesy National Portrait Gallery, London.

Louis XVIII in his study at the Tuileries by Baron Gérard (1824) Château de Versailles.

J.E. HUTCHINSON. R.T. WILSON. M. BRUCE.

John Hely-Hutchinson, Sir Robert Wilson and Michael Bruce by an unknown engraver (circa 1815).

Dorothy Jordan by John Russell (1792) Guildford Borough Council, Surrey, UK.
Courtesy The Bridgeman Art Library.

Caroline of Brunswick by James Lonsdale (1820).

The Earl of Aberdeen by John Partridge (1847). Courtesy National Portrait Gallery, London.

The entrance to the British Embassy, Paris.
Photograph © Queen's Printer and Controller of HMSO, 2005.
Courtesy UK Government Art Collection.

Lord Stuart de Rothesay's Highcliffe, now Highcliffe Castle.

James de Rothschild by Moritz Oppenheim.

8

In Parenthesis: The Escape of Lavalette 1815

The escape of the Comte de Lavalette from the prison of the Conciergerie, the day before he was to have been executed, is one of the romantic stories of the Second Restoration. Charles Stuart was suspected of having been involved in the conspiracy: he always maintained that he had had nothing to do with it, but a whiff of connivance, if not complicity, lingered on the air for some time. Lavalette had been Napoleon's Postmaster-General, with responsibility for the so-called Cabinet-Noir, the equivalent of the secret departments of the Post Office in London. His wife was the niece of the former Empress Joséphine.

Lavalette was one of the servants of Napoleon of whom the ultraroyalists were determined to make examples, though some of them had friends in high places, and were given the opportunity to leave the country before they could be arrested. The best known of them, Marshal Ney, was supplied with at least two passports, in different names, by Fouché,[1] who was briefly Minister of Police under Louis XVIII as he had been under Napoleon. But Ney was slow to make use of them, and was arrested and brought to trial on a charge of treason. A popular campaign to save him failed, in spite of appeals to Louis and the Prince Regent, and he was executed.

Lavalette's particular offence was to have taken over the

Post Office for Napoleon at the beginning of the Hundred Days, when Louis XVIII had already left Paris. The sentence of death was passed on 28 November, and an appeal against it was rejected on 14 December, between which dates, on 7 December, Ney was executed. Madame de Lavalette begged for her husband's life on her knees to the King, but His Majesty, who had done his best to avoid such a scene, told her that he could do nothing. The Comte and Comtesse were then thrown back on their own resources, which proved to be not inconsiderable.

Lavalette's execution was to have taken place on 22 December, and on 21 December the Comtesse paid what was supposedly her last visit to him. She had smuggled in a set of her clothes, which he put on, and while she made distracting noises behind a screen he walked out of the cell and out of the prison. One account has it that he left the Conciergerie on the arm of a prison officer.[2] Friends conducted him to a safe house, which happened to be an apartment in the Ministry of Foreign Affairs, and here he stayed, to the later embarrassment of the minister, the Duc de Richelieu, until plans could be made for him to leave France.

The Princesse de Vaudémont was a key figure in the conspiracy, and at this stage of its progress she recruited Michael Bruce, an English playboy, who had recommended himself to her by his support for the campaign to save Ney. Bruce is otherwise known to history as the one-time lover of the eccentric Lady Hester Stanhope, and at this time, ironically, he was involved in a relationship of gallantry if not intimacy with Mme la Maréchale Ney. He, in turn, recruited the maverick General Sir Robert Wilson, and together they brought in Captain John Hely-Hutchinson, of the 1st Regiment of Foot Guards (Grenadiers).

Bruce was known to Charles as a member of the group that he had led to safety from Madrid in December 1808,[3] if for no other reason. Wilson and Hely-Hutchinson's uncle, Lord

Hutchinson, were known to him as members of the party with which he had whiled away the time at Memel in the summer of 1807,[4] and Wilson had claimed his friendship since, whether properly or not.[5] Bruce and Wilson were both well known to the French Secret Police for their hostility to the Bourbon regime, but Hely-Hutchinson, whom Charles probably did not know, seems to have been politically innocent, which was an advantage to them all.

The plan decided on by the conspirators, put most simply, was that Lavalette should be disguised as a British officer, and that Wilson and Hely-Hutchinson, in their military uniforms, should escort him to the Belgian border. They left Paris on 10 January 1816, and all went according to plan, in spite of the fact that Bruce and Wilson were being watched by the Secret Police. Unfortunately, however, Wilson was then stupid enough, or vain enough, as Bruce had it,[6] to write a full account of the affair to his friend Lord Grey, and the letter was intercepted and copied for Decazes, who had replaced Fouché as Minister of Police.

In this particular letter, Wilson told Grey that he had obtained passports in assumed names for himself and Lavalette, with no questions asked, from Charles: 'I had no difficulty in procuring passports at my demand and on my own responsibility',[7] is the phrase he used, whatever can be inferred from it. In another intercepted letter to Grey, at about the same time, he made matters worse by expatiating on Charles' 'liberality and humanity' and he admitted later that, in doing so, he had compromised the Ambassador.[8] Castlereagh was shown these letters, perhaps with other information, and he was angry: he had been put at a disadvantage with the French government, notwithstanding Richelieu's embarassment, and with the Opposition in Parliament, of which Grey was a prominent member.

When Charles was first called on by Castlereagh to give an account of himself, he denied any wrongdoing as far as the passports were concerned but went on to acknowledge that he had sometimes let his tongue run away with him, and there is no doubt that he had laid himself open to suspicion: 'I do not suppose that the remaining observations respecting my feelings in favour of La Valette [*sic*] and my desire to prevent his arrestation create a more favourable impression on Your Lordship than they have done on the Duke de Richelieu,' he wrote on 7 March.[9] But if he thought that would be the end of the matter he had reckoned without Wilson.

Wilson, Bruce and Hely-Hutchinson had been arrested. They were tried for their offence, after far-fetched talk of capital charges, and sent to prison for three months. To Charles' relief, the subject of the passports was not raised at the trial.[10] But when Wilson returned to England, in an attempt to rehabilitate himself in the eyes of his Commander-in-Chief, the Duke of York, who took the view that he had disgraced his uniform, he repeated all that he had told Grey and hinted at more. The Duke was not impressed with Wilson, but he made sure that Castlereagh was informed of what had transpired.[11]

Now Castlereagh demanded the truth.[12] Was the passport used by Lavalette issued with Charles' 'privity, consent and knowledge of the person for whom it was intended?' And had Charles ever said anything to anyone 'which might be understood to give countenance to a British subject becoming the instrument of assisting a French subject to escape the public justice of his country?' Charles replied to the first question in the negative, for himself and his staff.[13] In reply to the second question, he asserted that he had never said anything about Lavalette except as part of 'the consideration of the effects his execution or pardon might produce upon the interests of the French Government'.[14]

Shortly afterwards, he reported to Castlereagh on a meeting with Wellington, at which had been discussed the hints dropped by Wilson for the benefit of the Duke of York.[15] He understood that Wilson had talked of 'persons who might be

60

involved unofficially if the part they bore in these transactions should be divulged', and he further understood that this phrase had been taken to be yet another reference to himself and the passports. Again, he denied any wrongdoing, and this time he expressed some indignation: there had, indeed, been fraud, but he had been one of the victims of it. He believed that the person whom Wilson had in mind was the Princesse de Vaudémont.

The story has no satisfactory conclusion. In an exchange of letters in August 1816, Charles asked Wilson to state categorically, once and for all, whether or not he regarded him as implicated in the Lavalette affair,[16] and Wilson was evasive.[17] He did not intend to divulge all he knew about the affair, he said: 'At the same time, I owe it to Your Excellency to state that I never communicated to Your Excellency any circumstances connected with the proposition which was made to me to save Lavallette [*sic*] until after my release from prison'.

9

In Parenthesis: Royal Errands 1816

The private papers of Mrs Jordan became the subject of anxious speculation in royal circles when she died on 5 July 1816, in France. Dora Jordan was a celebrated actress, who lived with the Duke of Clarence for twenty years and bore him ten children. He left her in 1811, having provided for her and their children as he saw fit; but, later, when she fell on hard times, he did nothing to help her. In 1814, she went to live at Boulogne, to escape her creditors, accompanied only by the children's former governess, a Miss Sketchley. She finally settled at Saint-Cloud, outside Paris. She did not live to see the Duke married to a German princess, Adelaide of Saxe-Meiningen, and later succeed to the throne as William IV.

The accounts of Mrs Jordan's death and funeral make sad reading, and the funeral would have been a more pathetic occasion than it was if it had not been for the intervention of an English resident of Paris, a Mr Greatorex, who took the arrangements out of Miss Sketchley's hands. None of Mrs Jordan's children was there, and the small congregation seems to have been made up of Mr Greatorex's friends. An account by a self-styled 'confidential friend of the departed' has it that 'the Rev. Mr Foster, a resident Chaplain to the British Embassy' was asked to officiate but 'chanced either to be unwell, or unable to attend'.[1] The chaplain was the Reverend Edward Forster, and his difficulty may have been truly diplomatic: although Mrs Jordan lived in France as Mrs James,

Charles Stuart must have known who she was.

Claire Tomalin, in *Mrs Jordan's Profession*, writes that 'Dora was first denied Christian burial by the Catholic Church – as an actress and a Protestant', and that 'only by "the strenuous interference of an English gentleman of some weight" was she allowed to be placed in the Saint-Cloud Cemetery at all'.[2] The Englishman of most weight, indeed the gentleman of most weight of any nationality usually resident in France during this period was the Duke of Wellington, but he happened to be in England at the time.[3] Perhaps Charles is meant. If it was he, the fact that he was not identified by name is not surprising: he would have acted discreetly, whether he acted on instructions or on his own initiative.

Two months later, on 24 September, Castlereagh wrote privately to Charles to say that the Duke of Clarence wished to have steps taken to secure Mrs Jordan's papers, 'now sealed up at St. Cloud'. 'H.R.H. is very desirous that her Private Papers may not *for obvious reasons* fall into improper hands,' the Foreign Secretary added.[4] By this time, Claire Tomalin tells us, Miss Sketchley had returned to England and obscurity, possibly with Mrs Jordan's diamond ring and certainly with the last instalment of her allowance;[5] and the words 'sealed up' suggest that the papers were supposedly being held by some official body. No doubt Charles did his best to oblige His Royal Highness, but he was unable to deliver the goods.

A year later, on 8 September 1817, Charles wrote to Castlereagh to report on further efforts to find the papers. (The 'Mr Macleay' of the letters was probably William Sharp Macleay, a young lawyer.[6])

Mr. Macleay called here yesterday to acquaint me with the result of his endeavours to procure any letters and papers which may have been in the possession of Mrs. Jordan at the time of her decease. He has found private papers and bills of trifling importance, together with the copy of a deed by which H.R.H. the Duke of Clarence settles an annuity on Mrs. Jordan during her life. If the private papers from H.R.H. were not destroyed by Mrs Jordan before her decease it is presumable under the circumstances that they remain in the possession of Mrs. Sketchley who resided with Mrs. Jordan as Dame de Compagnie and who returned to England immediately after her death.[7]

It may be that they were all wasting their time. Claire Tomalin has shown that Mrs Jordan returned all but a few of His Royal Highness's letters to him – or to a friend of his, who was supposed to put them safely into his hands – in 1811.[8] It may be, however, that it was the few letters that she did *not* return about which he was most concerned.

Soon after the death of Mrs Jordan, as it happened, Charles was asked to make discreet enquiries into another matter that threatened royal embarrassment. It appeared that certain packages addressed to the Prince Regent, and delivered first to the British embassy in Paris, had gone astray. These, according to a Foreign Office clerk, writing on behalf of one of the Prince's confidants, Benjamin Bloomfield, contained 'articles of dress *highly contraband*', which were intended as presents from His Royal Highness to Princess Charlotte and the Duchess of Gloucester.[9] The outcome of this investigation is not recorded.

10

The Affair of Queen Caroline and The Second Restoration 1819–1824

Two events, one in England and the other in France, dominated by their consequences Charles' private and secret work during the second half of his first term as Ambassador at Paris: in January 1820 George III died, and the accession of the Prince Regent as George IV made his wife, Caroline, Queen of England; in February 1820 the Duc de Berri, second in line of succession to the French throne, was assassinated, and public reaction brought power to the ultraroyalists. To complicate matters, Charles and his fellow diplomats soon had to contend with the consequences of another death, that of Castlereagh, in 1822, when Canning became Foreign Secretary again. And, to complicate matters further, neither George IV nor Canning was well known or trusted by the sovereigns and statesmen of Europe.

The Prince of Wales' marriage to Caroline of Brunswick had been a disaster from the first, and for several years the Princess had been living a fast life abroad. Now that they were King and Queen, he wished to be rid of her, but his ministers were anxious to avoid a divorce since, in the process, as much mud would stick to him as to her. There was also the possibility that, in a situation in which the radical element in British politics was to be reckoned with, the monarchy itself would suffer. Charles Stuart was drawn into the affair officially as one of the King's ministers abroad, and unofficially as a private investigator.

The King, when Prince of Wales and Regent, had taken care to collect information about his wife's behaviour that could be used against her in divorce proceedings. In 1818, when she was living at Pesaro, in Italy, he had sent a team of lawyers to Milan to interview potential witnesses. Caroline was aware of all this, and in 1819 she planned to return to England to challenge him. Henry Brougham, her chief legal adviser, counselled caution, and they agreed to meet at Lyons to discuss her position. Charles well knew that her return would be unwelcome to the Prince and his ministers, and when he heard that she would be travelling through France he made sure of clear instructions from Castlereagh. These instructions were that Caroline was simply not to be given any special attention as Princess of Wales.[1]

Caroline kept the rendezvous at Lyons, but – to her disgust – Brougham did not. She turned back, instead of travelling on; and it was at Leghorn (Livorno) that she learned that she was Queen. Brougham now urged her to return to England at once, but some weeks passed before she was ready to set out again. The stakes had been raised, and attitudes had hardened. Castlereagh suggested to Charles that he should find some way of preventing her from crossing the Channel, perhaps with the help of the French police,[2] but if he tried he did not succeed and we know nothing about it. Brougham, who was playing a double game, met her at St Omer, and she crossed the Channel on 5 June 1820.

Caroline was determined that she should be recognised as Queen, but the King was equally determined that she should not. It soon became clear that no compromise was possible. The government then resorted to an old parliamentary manoeuvre, a Bill of Pains and Penalties, the second reading of which would be tantamount to a trial; and, if passed by both Houses of Parliament, this would deprive Caroline of her status as Queen and end her marriage to the King. An important factor in the case against her would be her relationship with one Bartolemeo Pergami, an Italian whom she had engaged as a courier and then promoted rapidly until, having bought for him an estate in Sicily with which went the title of Baron, and thus made him a nominal gentleman, she had appointed him her chamberlain. It was believed that they were lovers.

Much time and money had already been expended on the Pergami factor when Charles became involved with it. Lord Clanwilliam, acting Under-Secretary at the Foreign Office, wrote to him on 27 June:

> You will probably, among the rumours of the day, have heard that Pergami accompanied the Queen to Calais: and it is also stated that he thence returned to Paris. Should this latter report prove correct it is wished that he should be a little *looked* after, and that it should be known what he is about.[3]

Charles arranged to have Pergami watched by the police until he left Paris in July,[4] and evidently heard nothing about him that he thought worthy of being passed on. But this was not the end of the matter for Charles. It was being said that Caroline's lawyers were to claim that Pergami was impotent, and Clanwilliam wrote to Charles again on 12 September:

> I am therefore directed confidentially to call Your Excellency's attention to this report, and to request you to use your endeavours for discovering whether, during Pergami's stay in Paris, he did not keep a certain *Mlle Legros*, and some other woman: in short whether his sojourn there cannot produce evidence of his virility.[5]

They were unusual instructions, and they proved difficult to follow.

Charles was ready with a certain amount of information within a week, however, and in a reply to Clanwilliam, dated 18 September,[6] he recounted a story that he had recently been told by Berkeley Craven, brother of Keppel Craven, one of Caroline's vice-chamberlains. Keppel Craven had heard it said among Caroline's servants that Pergami had been castrated, and he questioned the Italian on the subject. Pergami, 'without hesitation, said that he had suffered much from the cold on the retreat from Russia and that his scrotum had been partly if not entirely frostbitten'.

This is not a story that would have been likely to impress expert medical witnesses as proof or evidence of impotence, particularly as caricatures and cartoons of the time show Pergami with a healthy growth of facial hair. Frostbite affects chiefly the nose, ears, fingers and toes, and frostbite of the scrotum would be an unusual injury. If such an injury did occur, the contents of the scrotum would not necessarily be affected, since they have a separate blood supply. If both the scrotum and its contents were affected, and virtual castration were the result, hair growth would be much reduced, though not stopped. It is true, of course, that castration usually results in impotence.

In the same letter, Charles dealt with the question of the women mentioned by Clanwilliam. Mlle Legros was a well-known actress, and any connection between her and Pergami would have been the talk of the town. As far as the 'other woman' was concerned, it was said that Pergami had lived with a certain 'Aurelia', but the story could not be confirmed. Charles went on:

He certainly did pay two visits to the celebrated Mme Auguste in consequence of receiving the usual invitation which is addressed to strangers from houses of that description, but he did not give any proof of his virility upon those occasions. He went there once apparently from motives of curiosity, and returned mainly for the purpose of introducing an Italian whom he stated to be his particular friend.

The next letter that Charles received from the Foreign Office was written by Joseph Planta on 30 September,[7] and in it Planta referred to a letter from Charles of 25 September. This letter has not come to light, but it evidently contained the information that Pergami was known to have lived with a Mme Ebênes in Paris; and Planta told Charles that the Prime Minister himself, Lord Liverpool, was anxious to be assured that this relationship at least was sexual: 'It would not be necessary to prove the fact of adultery', Planta quoted Liverpool as having said, 'but that he placed himself in such a position in relation to the person, as to make the object of his so doing manifest'.

But still there was no proof. Charles' last letter in the series is dated 3 October,[8] and it has an almost apologetic tone. He had had several agents working on the case, and there was no doubt that Pergami had lived with the lady; on the other hand, there was no evidence that she had provided him with more than board and lodging. She was under some obligation to him for kindnesses shown to her husband and children in Italy, and the inference was that her husband had no complaint about the arrangement. Charles went on to refer to Pergami's daughter, Vittorine, and noted that she was probably born – or at least conceived – before the retreat from Moscow. However, it is said that Vittorine had a younger sister.[9]

The trial duly took place, but it had an inconclusive ending. It was never claimed on Carolina's behalf that Pergami was impotent, and it was generally agreed that she had committed adultery with him and others; but it was equally generally agreed that her treatment at the hands of the King and his ministers, particularly as regards the way in which the case against her had been built up, was only a little less reprehensible. The bill was given embarrassingly weak support, and it was withdrawn. But Caroline was never given the recognition that she craved, and she died less than a year later.

The assassination of the Duc de Berri, sad as it was for his family – not least because he did not live to see his son and heir, the Duc de Bordeaux – had unhappy consequences for all of France. It destroyed the political balance kept by the royalists by giving extra weight to the claims of the ultraroyalists, and in so doing it provoked a confrontation between the right and the left. Now was the day of the secret revolutionary societies, which had caused trouble in Naples and Spain. Plots were hatched in various parts of the country, chiefly in garrison towns, where discontented soldiers were to be found, but all were uncovered in time, largely as a result of the infiltration of the societies by the Secret Police. According to one historian, 'the most active plotters seem to have been police spies, paid by results'.[10]

The political consequences of the assassination were felt in England, too. A revolution in Spain in 1820 gave power to liberals and forced Ferdinand VII to forswear absolute monarchy, and a botched counter-revolution in 1822 left the King helpless. Ultraroyalists in France took up his cause, and Britain, as represented by Canning, though unimpressed by the Spanish form of constitutional monarchy and wary of political ideology, saw a more serious threat in the pretensions of absolute monarchs and extreme royalists than in the opposing forces of change. At the Congress at Verona, in 1822, the danger of French military intervention became clear, and Canning and his colleagues had to consider Britain's options, one of which was war.

Espionage was not a matter to which the Foreign Office liked to refer directly. Six years earlier, however, Castlereagh had sent Charles clear instructions to spy on the French Navy:

I am to desire that you will use all possible diligence and

discretion in obtaining and transmitting to me the fullest
account of the present state in numbers force and condi-
tion of the fleets and squadrons of France, together with
the estimated quantity of timber and stores in the several
arsenals, and the number of docks and ships of the
several classes, and the amount of manual labour at
present employed in the arsenals, and that you should
continue from time to time your information on these
points, being careful to notice all the changes that may
have taken place since the date of the last communication
you may have made thereon.[11]

To digress, when, one day in 1822, Castlereagh was
challenged in Parliament by Joseph Hume on the subject of
expenditure on the Secret Services, he rose splendidly to the
occasion. It happened to be 1 April:

If the hon. member wished to know the amount expended under this head in former years, he might have an
account of the expenditure in each year for the last eleven
years; but if he wished to know the particular details of
how it was expended, it was rather an Irish proposition,
for it would then be secret service money no longer.[12]

To return to the story, assuming that Charles followed his
instructions from Castlereagh the British government must
have been in possession of a considerable amount of information about the French Navy when the Spanish crisis arose in
1822. When the crisis was about to reach its climax, in 1823,
Charles was able to supply a significant amount of information
about the French Army as well. This came from the British
Consul in Bordeaux,[13] and Canning noted that he received it
from Charles in a private letter, presumably to register the
point that it had not been included in an official dispatch for
security reasons. Both dispatches and letters were more than

ever liable to be intercepted, and while Charles took his own precautions he advised couriers from Madrid, who usually travelled through Paris, to vary their route.[14]

The French Army invaded Spain and occupied the country, and Ferdinand's rule was given a new lease of life. Canning had deliberately left France guessing as to his government's intentions for as long as possible, but neither he nor any of his colleagues wanted Britain to have to fight for Spain, while both George IV and Wellington might have preferred to fight for France, and neutrality was the option that was chosen. This was taken as a diplomatic defeat for Canning, but France was warned, in an unusually public manner, that Britain would remain neutral only if there were, first, no permanent French occupation of Spain and, secondly, no French threat to Portugal or any of the Spanish and Portuguese colonies in South America.

The warning was taken seriously, and Canning and Wellington together monitored developments in Spain. Though Wellington sympathised with France, to the extent that he did not like to see legitimate authority overthrown, as it had been in Spain, he well knew that limits had to be set. As far as Portugal was concerned, in any case, he was unlikely to have forgotten that Britain was bound by ancient defence treaties. The monitoring process was assisted by Charles, who provided reports on the distribution and strength of French military units in Spain.[15] By putting together current intelligence and his knowledge of the Peninsula, Wellington was able to second-guess French strategy.[16] Fortunately, it was, in the end, possible for Britain to avoid war with France.

We do not know how Charles obtained his information from Spain. He may have been able to make use of contacts that he had made during the Peninsular War. It is also possible that Wood or Alonzo took a hand. There is little mention of Wood in the records for these years, but he was with Charles at the embassy, and he was well-known and well-liked there. Lord

Granville referred to him as *maître d'hôtel*, and arranged for him to remain as such, if only temporarily, when he succeeded Charles as Ambassador in 1824.[17] Wellington entrusted him with various personal commissions.[18]

Payments from Charles' Separate Account with Coutts & Co. in London, and from this to his account with Bagenault & Co. in Paris, continued to be made. Among the entries in the accounts between 1819 and 1824 are three that, taken together, are particularly interesting: on 11 November 1823, a sum of £6000 was paid into the Separate Account by Nathan Rothschild; and on 19 January and again on 4 February 1824, sums of £3000 were paid from that account to Rothschild & Co.[19] Thus £6000 was paid in and paid back within a period of four months. A letter from J.C. Herries, Financial Secretary to the Treasury, to Nathan Rothschild, on behalf of Frederick Robinson, Chancellor of the Exchequer, on 3 November 1823, may explain this:

Mr. Robinson desires I will state to you that H.E. Sir Charles Stuart is in want of a sum of between five and six thousand pounds at Paris, and I am to request you to place this sum at Sir Charles Stuart's disposal and to inform you that it will be replaced about the month of April next.

P.S. The sum in question is required to defray the expenses of repairs to the Ambassador's house at Paris.[20]

But this was the period at which the situation in Spain was keeping the Secret Service busy, and the repairs to the Ambassador's house may have made a cover story. The transaction seems a strange one, and all the more so for the fact that no reference to it has been found in the Rothschild Archive.[21]

11

Interlude 1824–1828

The greater part of the years 1825 and 1826 were spent by Charles in Portugal and Brazil. Britain was asked to mediate between the two countries in their negotiations over Brazil's independence of Portugal, and Canning chose Charles to lead the mission. It was a successful one, but no sooner had the treaty of independence been signed and ratified than Dom João, King of Portugal, died and Dom Pedro, Emperor of Brazil, inherited the crown of Portugal. Pedro now renounced his Portuguese inheritance in favour of Donna Maria da Gloria, his eldest daughter, who was still a child; but, at the same time, he gave Portugal a new constitution and persuaded Charles to deliver the constitutional documents when he returned from South America to Europe. Charles had been given Portuguese diplomatic status for his mission, and he took the view that Pedro's word was his command.

The new constitution caused outrage in ultraroyal and non-constitutional circles in Portugal and in the rest of Europe, and Canning was hard put to it to convince critics that Charles had not acted with his knowledge and consent. This was bad enough, but Charles made matters worse by a piece of interference in Portugal's internal affairs for which he had an explanation but no excuse. Pedro had made the Infanta Isabel Maria, his sister, Regent for the young Maria da Gloria, and it was to Isabel Maria that Charles delivered the constitutional documents. Portugal had been thrown into a state of turmoil

77

by what was known and what was rumoured about the constitution, and by the manoeuvrings of Dom Miguel, Pedro's ultraroyalist brother, who claimed the throne for himself. Isabel Maria cast Charles in the role of confidant and adviser, which he was unwise enough tacitly to accept.[1]

While Canning was Foreign Secretary from 1822 to 1827 the Secret Service flourished, so that, for instance, he could claim to know as much about French agents in South America as did the French Minister for Foreign Affairs.[2] He seems also to have kept an eye, by proxy, on his own men. The papers of Lord Howard de Walden, an Under-Secretary at the Foreign Office, whom Canning sent as an attaché on Charles' mission, contain copies of the letters of British and foreign diplomats, some deciphered or translated, and among them are copies of a number of Charles' private letters. What we know about Charles' private and secret activities in these years relates chiefly to the first stage of his mission, in Portugal, and it comes in part from the Howard de Walden Papers.[3]

There was much suspicion of Britain's motives in agreeing to mediate between Portugal and Brazil: it was supposed, not unnaturally, that she wished to extend her influence in South America, and other countries with interests in the continent, such as Spain and France, began to invest heavily in intelligence and intrigue. Portugal was divided on the question of Britain's involvement in the independence negotiations but also, more fundamentally, divided on the question of independence; and it was at Lisbon that intrigue had most to be reckoned with.

At Lisbon, in April and May 1825, Charles conferred with Dom João and his Foreign Minister, the Conde de Porto Santo, supported by the British Ambassador, Sir William a'Court. He told his wife that Dom João was particularly fond of him,[4] and he certainly obtained from the King and the Count an agreement that allowed him to move on to the second stage of his mission, in Brazil. But, experienced though he was, he may have been deceived by flattery. A'Court reported to Canning that His Majesty's confidence in Charles was being systematically undermined by a group of his advisers,[5] who were encouraging him to believe that the mission was a cover for a quite different scheme concerning the Queen.

Queen Carlota Joaquina was confined to the pink palace at Queluz as punishment for having supported Dom Miguel in an attempt to seize the throne, the latest in a series of offences, including adultery and complicity in murder, which marked her marriage. Dom João believed that the mission's real object was her rehabilitation.[6] False as this belief was, however, Charles unwittingly played into the hands of the intrigants by taking too close an interest in her. Indeed, in a letter to his old friend Marshal Beresford, a copy of which is among the Howard de Walden Papers, he claimed so to have arranged matters that she had been permitted to see her husband and make a fresh plea for liberty, though he admitted that nothing had been said to Carlota Joaquina or to him that justified optimism on this score.[7]

He also took an interest in Beresford's affairs in Portugal. The Marshal had commanded the Portuguese Army during the Peninsular war and afterwards, and had served the country well, but a revolution while he was visiting Brazil in 1820 had left him *persona non grata*. Charles now raised with the King the questions of his freedom to return to Portugal and his right to certain property in the country, and this time he had good news to pass on: 'Upon the whole' he wrote in the same letter, 'matters look better; the wind is changing, and many of those who were not disposed to wish for your return have begun to desire it'.[8] As far as the property was concerned, the King had simply decreed that it was Beresford's.

Charles' letter to Beresford showed Canning that he was not minding his own business at Lisbon, and that must have been bad enough, but there was other intercepted correspondence, concerning Charles, that alarmed and angered the Foreign

Secretary. There were several letters from the Prussian Minister at Lisbon, M. de Royer, to his King, reporting the opinions of Canning's South American policy said to have been expressed by Charles and a'Court. Both diplomats were alleged to be highly critical of their own government's policy, and to be personally ultraroyal and anti-constitutional by persuasion.[9] Canning wrote a private letter to a'Court, which has not come to light but evidently suggested that the two had taken leave of their senses, and Charles responded to it with great indignation:

> In answer to this letter I can only assure you that I have not lost my senses, and that I think it extremely unfair that you should receive such an impression from the correpondence of a person with whom, by your own order, I have abstained from communicating upon political subjects.
>
> I must also assure you that if I had disapproved your measures with respect to Spanish and Portuguese America I could not, consistently with my own feelings, have accepted employment for the express purpose of advancing, by every effort in my power, the system of policy which you think it is expedient for the King's Government to adopt ...

And he added as a postscript:

> The public of this country do not entertain the opinion of my sentiments which is expressed in your letter to Sir William a'Court, for I am assured that my health, coupled with the manifestation of their wish for a constitutional government, was drunk at several of the public meetings which took place in Lisbon yesterday in honour of the King of Portugal's birthday.[10]

A'Court's response was even stronger.

80

I never was more surprised in my life, than by the receipt of your private and confidential letter of 30th April.

The tone in which it is written makes me hope, indeed, that you place no great faith in M.de Royer's reports. There is something consolatory, too, in finding that Sir Charles Stuart has been subjected to the same accusation as myself, for tho' you might have believed that *one* person was gone mad, upon M.de Royer's assertion, you would naturally hesitate in giving credit to a similar charge against *two*.

I need hardly say that the insinuation of M.de Royer is totally unfounded. My profession of faith upon the American question may be gathered from my dispatches, as well as from my private letters, and I may add that it has never varied. By a reference to my Madrid correspondence, you will see that on 8th January, 1823, *long before you had come to a decision upon the question*, I recommended an immediate acknowledgement of the independence of the Spanish colonies, as the safest mode of frustrating the secret machinations of France. I have never had a doubt of the policy of the measure; I have never ceased to defend it; and, as the agent of Great Britain, I have worked furtherance of your views to the best of my ability.[11]

There is a mystery here. Was the Prussian minister to be believed, in spite of Charles' and a'Court's protestations, or was he making mischief, knowing that his letters would be intercepted? False information was certainly disseminated in this way. It is possible that one but not the other of the British diplomats had been foolish and indiscreet. Canning appears to have accepted a'Court's denial straightaway;[12] but, later, in a letter to his friend Lord Granville, he referred to all Charles' correspondence at Lisbon – without explaining, or perhaps not needing to explain, how he knew so much about it – as having been written 'in the highest strain of Ultraism'.[13] Then, later still, he found himself having to account to ultraroyalists for Charles' part in furnishing Portugal with its new constitution. No wonder Canning found Charles infuriating.

If Charles had been foolish and indiscreet, a'Court would have been aware of the fact, and though he might have wished to defend or protect him from Canning's wrath he would have been unlikely to go as far as he did in a final report to the Foreign Secretary on their work together at Lisbon:

> I am sure it will be a satisfaction to you to know, that the most cordial harmony and good understanding has existed between us during the whole of his mission, and that we have laboured together for the same objects, tho' in our separate walks, with a goodwill which has proved as advantageous to H.M.'s service as to our reputations and characters here.

And, drawing attention to the intrigue that had complicated the mission at Lisbon, he added: 'The wish to sow division between us existed to the fullest force, but every effort made for that purpose proved altogether unavailing'.[14]

Britain is unlikely to have had cleaner hands than any of her potential enemies, of course. We know that Canning made much use of the Secret Service, and that he had letters intercepted without scruple, but our information otherwise is scanty. This makes one of a'Court's letters to Canning, from Lisbon, on 23 May 1825, at the end of Charles' stay, particularly tantalizing:

> I have the honour to acknowledge the receipt of your secret and separate dispatch authorising me to pay Sir Augustus West a sum not exceeding £200 annually from the period of my arrival in this country, and to charge the same on my secret service account.[15]

82

Charles still had friends in Portugal, dating back to the Peninsular War. Indeed, it was partly because he was known and trusted at Lisbon that Canning had chosen him as mediator. No doubt some of these friends were able to provide him with useful information, officially or unofficially, and one who is likely to have contributed on a confidential basis was the Condessa d'Amadia. Violet Stuart Wortley, who edited some of Charles' papers, certainly believed that she did:

> The Countess was very much behind the scenes in official life in Portugal, and was able to keep him *au courant* in regard to the complicated relations existing between Portugal and Brazil. This was very useful to Stuart, when in 1826 he was sent on a mission to Brazil.[16]

Louis Casamajor, Chargé d'Affaires at Lisbon briefly during the summer of 1814, told Charles that life there was not the same without him: 'The Countess is quite inconsolable', he reported.[17] Violet Stuart Wortley notes:

> The lady alluded to is the Countess Amadia, whose devotion to and correspondence with Charles Stuart continued many years after he had quitted Portugal. Her letters would furnish a history of her country's politics if they were decipherable; unfortunately, she and Charles Stuart wrote almost illegibly, though voluminously.[18]

Charles was away from England from the spring of 1825 until the autumn of 1826, and he returned with his achievement in Brazil overshadowed by his indiscretion in Portugal. If he had not been the bearer of the constitutional documents from Brazil to Portugal, or even if, having delivered those documents, he had not remained in the country as the Regent's confidant and adviser, all might have been well. As it was, however, he was received at the Foreign Office coolly, if not icily, and the elevation to the peerage for which he had hoped, as reward for the undoubted success of his official mission, was blocked by Canning.

Canning became Prime Minister in April 1827, and Charles must have assumed that his career would progress no further, but in August of the same year Canning died. He was succeeded as Prime Minister by Viscount Goderich, who, in January 1828, made way for the Duke of Wellington. Goderich was related both to Charles and to Charles' wife, and he recommended a peerage for Charles. Wellington confirmed the recommendation, and in January 1828 Charles became 1st Baron Stuart de Rothesay of the Isle of Bute. There was talk of his becoming Foreign Secretary,[19] but, whether or not this was serious talk, his appointment as Ambassador at Paris, for a second term, is likely to have been more congenial to him. His credentials were dated 1 July 1828.[20]

12

Charles Stuart and Lord Aberdeen 1828–1831

Lord Aberdeen's first term as Foreign Secretary coincided with Charles' second term as Ambassador at Paris. Castlereagh and Canning had both taken a special interest in the Secret Service, but relatively little is known about Aberdeen's attitude towards it; what is known is that he was no less realistic or worldly a man than either Castlereagh or Canning. He was happy to leave the secret department of the Post Office to its own devices, and he was unfazed by duplicity.[1] He made as much use of private letters as any of his predecessors or successors; and one result of this was that a considerable amount of sensitive information never found its way into the official records,[2] a matter for which Charles was to have reason to be grateful.

Charles arrived in Paris on 19 July 1828, and presented his credentials on 15 August.[3] By 25 August he had settled back into his old job comfortably enough to write to Aberdeen, privately, about the possibility of manipulating the French press to Britain's advantage.[4] The editors of several Paris-based papers had offered to sell their influence to him during his first term, and now, already, at the beginning of his second, one editor had made an offer and another seemed likely to want to do business. Aberdeen was interested, and he replied to Charles with one of his own private letters on 2 September.[5] The definite offer depended on harmless favours, rather than cash payments, and so could be taken up as soon as Charles saw fit. There was more at stake in the other case, since the paper concerned was reprinting anti-French articles from the London press, but Charles was to do nothing, at that stage, except make discreet enquiries as to the cost of doing business.

Meanwhile, on 29 August, Charles had written to Aberdeen again, in a letter marked 'secret' rather than simply 'private'.[6] First, he referred to a complaint that the Austrian Ambassador at Paris had made to the French Minister of Foreign Affairs, about the way his country was being treated by the Paris press. Charles had learned of this from a confidential letter from Metternich to the Minister, which he must have seen; but he said nothing about how he had come by it, presumably because the interception of letters was so much a matter of routine. Next, he referred to certain reports from his agents, which had been or were to be forwarded to Aberdeen, to show that he was, himself, already checking out the Paris press.

Charles went on, in the same letter, to discuss two agents whom he had taken over with the embassy: Mr Darby and Mr Goldsmith. Evidently, he was not pleased with either, and if this was the Mr Darby who had been sent back to England in 1822,[7] he was now to be sent back for the second time. Mr Goldsmith was to remain, perhaps because he had influential friends, but Charles wished it to be understood that he was responsible to the embassy and not to the Foreign Office:

There have been hitherto two individuals at Paris in the pay of Government, a Mr. Darby and a Mr. Goldsmith. As the former was merely the channel through whom an inferior agent transmitted reports, which I propose in future to receive directly, I have resolved to give him a small gratuity previous to his return to England which will shortly take place.

Mr. Goldsmith, however, being in the habit of addres-

86

sing letters to the Under-Secretary of State reporting his own communications with the French Minister, I requested Mr. Backhouse to let me know the nature of the instructions under which he acted and that gentleman has informed me that Mr. Goldsmith was ordered by the Secretary of State 'to make himself useful in obtaining information which he should communicate under flying seal to His Majesty's Ambassador'.

I submit to you, if under these circumstances, it would not be more decorous to place him under the orders of the Embassy and if you think his communications of any value, of which I must fairly tell you I entertain very considerable doubts, to direct him to report to me rather than the Foreign Office.

The reports of the inferior agent transmitted by Mr. Goldsmith are absolutely useless.

Annotations to the letter by the Under-Secretary, John Backhouse, show that he did not accept the implied criticism of him.

Aberdeen's response to what Charles had to say about the two agents, which came in a letter dated 2 September, is vague and suggests no great sense of involvement, but it has to be remembered that the new Foreign Secretary had not yet had time to become closely involved. His musings on the value to be attached to the sort of information that such agents provided make up the most interesting part of the letter, though Charles must have heard it all before:

With respect to our own Secret Reporters, I scarcely know what to say, for I know very little about them. At the same time I have been sometimes struck with the accurate information which they have conveyed. Mr. Goldsmith, who from being so well known as a political trader, it is difficult to imagine is in a very good position for communicating with persons in possession of much knowledge, certainly continues to send accounts of facts long before they are publickly known. I see no objection to his continuing to address the office as at present, sending of course everything open through your hands. Of the other person whom you are going to send to England, Mr. Darby, I know nothing at all, but his reports also frequently contain curious and not unimportant information. The evil of all such communications is that it is impossible to know what is true and what is false; their business is as well answered if they lie like truth. On the whole I am by no means inclined to place much reliance upon them; perhaps not so much as they deserve. I am quite sure it must be a very different medium however, which could justify any considerable expense in the pursuit of secret information.[8]

But Aberdeen soon became more definite and directive. The Eastern Question was occupying his thoughts towards the end of the year 1828. Turkey was losing its grip on its empire, and Greece was making a bid for freedom while Russia was looking for territorial gains. Britain and France were playing the part of honest brokers, but Britain was suspicious of France's honesty. It was in this context that certain information obtained by one of Charles' agents from the French Ministry of Foreign Affairs attracted the British Foreign Secretary's attention, and in a letter dated 20 November he asked for more:

I wish you to fathom a little more the report of a conversation stated to have taken place before la Ferronays and described in the last Secret Bulletin on Nov 16th. There is no doubt that France now holds the balance between us and Russia, and she is playing us off obviously against each other. I have had some misgivings of late, about the honesty of the Government, and certainly the conversation to which I allude is precisely such as would confirm my apprehension. What do you say about it? Is it accurately reported – or have you any dependence on your Reporter, and the accuracy of his information?[9]

We do not know exactly what information the original report contained, or what more Charles was able to provide.

In one of the collections of Charles' papers there is a letter addressed to 'Son Excellence Lord Stuart de Rothesay, Ambassadeur de la Grande Bretagne, En Son Hôtel à Paris'.[10] It is marked *'Très Pressée'* and also 'Very Hastened'. The writer, who identified himself only as a Frenchman, offered to pass to the Ambassador *'un secret d'état'* if he would send a carriage to a rendezvous later that day to meet him. Charles is likely to have been wary of this offer, which might have been worthless and might have been a trap, but he rarely erred on the side of caution in his decisions and he did not destroy the letter, two points that suggest that the rendezvous was kept.

The date on the letter is *'Samedi,* 27th March'. The year is not given, but it can only have been 1830, since Charles was Ambassador at Paris as Lord Stuart de Rothesay in the month of March only in 1829 and 1830, and 27 March was a Saturday in 1830 and not in 1829.

By this time, the great bone of contention between Britain and France was Algeria. France was planning what was ostensibly an expedition against the Barbary pirates but actually the invasion and annexation of Algeria, and Britain strongly suspected the truth. Perhaps the state secret that Charles was offered was this. 'We learned all from others before we heard a word from them', Wellington remarked to Aberdeen a month later, when the French could no longer keep up their pretence.[11]

Alonzo makes his last appearances in Charles' papers for

these years, and the references to him tell us a little more about him. It had been agreed that he should have an allowance from the Foreign Office between Charles' appointments,[12] but when it was discontinued in 1828 Charles complained: 'This person has been with me near twenty years and in circumstances of great importance' he told Aberdeen, 'and his merits were well known to Lord Castlereagh who employed him a great deal during his residence in Paris'.[13] When Charles was recalled in 1830, he did his best to provide for his servant by writing to the then Foreign Secretary, Lord Palmerston, on his behalf:

Your Lordship will, I hope, permit me to sollicit [*sic*] the protection of His Majesty's Government in favour of my secretary Mr. J. Roman Alonso, whose services to His Majesty's Government in my successive missions, embassies and congresses in Spain, Portugal, France, Holland and Brazil are well known at the Foreign Office.[14]

13

'A Most Scandalous Proceeding' 1828–1829

Smuggling and the misuse of the diplomatic bag were matters that a Foreign Secretary could sometimes afford to ignore, but it was soon after his appointment that Lord Aberdeen had to complain to Charles, for the first time, of what he called 'a most scandalous proceeding'.[1] Exactly what was involved on this occasion we do not know, but a letter from Aberdeen to Wellington, the Prime Minister, dated 9 December 1828, tells us something about it:

> I think it as well to send you my private letter to Stuart today. The case is really a bad one, otherwise you ought not to be troubled with it. The intercourse between the London and Paris shopkeepers, by means of the ambassador's bag, is constant, by the contrivance of this person who receives a percentage upon the things sent. It appears that his profit upon one expedition alone is a hundred pounds, and upon another two hundred pounds. This surely is beyond the reasonable limit of indulgence, and ought to be checked.[2]

A letter that he wrote Charles later shows that 'this person' was William Wood,[3] who nevertheless managed to keep his job.

Wood had returned to Charles' service when Charles had

91

returned to Paris. He had probably remained at the embassy for some time after Charles left it in 1824, as *maître d'hôtel* to Lord Granville,[4] but by 1826 he had begun a new career as a nurseryman, with land at Maresfield in Sussex.[5] Later there was a nursery in France, too, on the edge of Paris, not far from the embassy, and even at this stage, in 1826, Wood was importing and exporting plants and shrubs.[6] He came from a humble background,[7] and spent the first half of his working life as a servant, but was evidently a wealthy man when he came to buy land. The sources of his wealth are likely to have been espionage and smuggling.

On 2 October 1829, *The Times* reprinted an article from a Calais newspaper, headed 'Smuggling in the name of the English Ambassador'. Ten cases of goods had been unloaded from a vessel at Calais on 22 July, and had been sent on to Paris without customs formalities because they were addressed to the Ambassador. They had aroused the suspicion of customs officials at Paris, however, because they were said to contain household items of a kind with which it was thought the embassy must already be equipped. When opened, five cases were found to contain 'a large quantity of English goods, such as poplins, figured stuff for waistcoats, gilt articles, tobacco, varnished leather, etc.', and another two 'were filled with tulle [soft silk net] in pieces and bands'. These seven cases, together, weighed about one and a half tons.

Great indignation was expressed in the article, not all of it directed at the smuggling itself, though the smuggling of tulle certainly angered the people of Calais, many of whom depended for their livelihood on the manufacture of this material. There was a political angle: the British Prime Minister, Wellington, and the French Minister of Foreign Affairs, soon to be Chief Minister, Polignac, were both deeply unpopular in certain quarters, and Polignac was considered to have deferred too much to Wellington by allowing the cases of contraband to be returned to England, rather than having them confiscated. 'Calais is in alarm', the writer trumpeted, 'and in its indignation it asks what France has done that it should be governed by men who thus betray her dearest interests'.

Now Aberdeen had to complain to Charles for the second time, and he sent him a copy of the article on the day it appeared, with a request for his comments.[8] Charles' response has not been found, but it cannot have been satisfactory because Aberdeen wrote to him again a few days later, asking if he could give an assurance, on his word of honour, that whatever had been done in his name had been done without his knowledge.[9] The cases had arrived back in England, meanwhile, so that more had become known about their contents, which evidently included smaller packages, and Aberdeen continued, making himself clear in spite of his syntax:

> The names of the persons to whom articles were addressed on the packages now in our Customs House cover so very small a proportion of the whole quantity sent to Paris, and the remainder being ostensibly directed to you, with the participation of your known agents in the country in the affair render such a personal assurance highly desirable.

And, in this letter, too, Aberdeen drew attention to the fact that Wood was still being employed by Charles, referring to him as 'the servant whom you have so unaccountably protected'.

It has to be assumed that Charles was able to give Aberdeen the assurance for which he had asked, however difficult it may have been for him to do so. Wood became the scapegoat, whether rightly or wrongly, and whether willingly or unwillingly.[10] Two letters from Charles to Aberdeen on successive days, 26 and 27 October,[11,12] made up, to all intents and purposes, his final report, and though it was incomplete it

93

seems to have been allowed to close the episode. If the Foreign Secretary was satisfied, however, the Prime Minister was not: 'It is difficult for the Duke to believe Lord Stuart about the smuggling after learning what he has from other quarters', said Wellington, in a message to Aberdeen on 22 October.[13]

It is fair to conclude that in this case, as in the case of Lavalette, the story that emerged was not the truth, the whole truth and nothing but the truth. We do not know what Wellington knew; but we do know that Charles did not dismiss Wood until he was obliged to do so, and we know that they parted on good terms. Handed down in the Wood family, among other items that once belonged to William, has been an engraving of the Gérard portrait of Charles, inscribed by him, against the date 'October 1830', 'Presented to William Wood as a token of esteem for his faithful services during 30 years abroad'.[14] It may be relevant to note, too, that Wood was almost certainly supporting himself and his family from the profits of his nursery by this time.

Another piece of evidence suggests complicity or connivance with Wood's activities on Charles' part, though its significance is not clear, perhaps because it was not intended to be. This is a letter written by Wood, in London, to Charles, in Paris, on 29 August 1829.[15] Wood had crossed the Channel, apparently to oversee the dispatch of certain unspecified items to Charles, and something had gone wrong. Customs, whether British or French, was mentioned, and Wood said there was likely to be trouble and he might be involved in considerable expense, for which he was not prepared, if these items were not sent back to England.

Charles and Wood parted company at this stage in their careers. Wood's business thrived during his lifetime, and on his death in 1863 it passed to his son, Charles,[16] who was Charles Stuart's godson.[17] Young Charles also inherited the engraving of the Gérard portrait.[18] Wood left to his grandson, William Charles, a gun that had belonged to Napoleon, and to his

94

granddaughter, Mary Ann, china that had been part of a present from Napoleon to Marie Louise when they were married.[19] Other bequests, if without the same provenance or cachet, were mementos of an adventurous life.

14

Colonel Cradock 1830

The most dramatic and potentially the most disastrous of Charles' clandestine operations took place in 1830, in the setting of the revolution in Paris of that summer. The reactionary Comte d'Artois had succeeded his brother Louis XVIII as Charles X in 1824, and had shown no more interest in reigning as a constitutional monarch than had been expected of him. A political crisis followed hard on an economic crisis, and in an attempt to provide himself with an effective government the King resorted to a series of ordinances, which would have had the effect of rigging elections and muzzling the press. In the Three Glorious Days of 27, 28 and 29 July, the people of Paris rose against the government and the King, and were joined by defectors from the civil and military forces sent to restore order.

Early on 29 July, Marshal Marmont, commanding the troops, warned Polignac, the King's unpopular Chief Minister, that he would not be able to control the situation if the ordinances that had so roused the people were not withdrawn; but Polignac thought he knew better. The King was at Saint-Cloud, outside Paris, and one account has it that Charles and the Russian Ambassador, Pozzo di Borgo, went together to alert him to the danger he faced, but were not allowed to see him.[1] Finally that day, some of the King's ministers succeeded in persuading him to revoke the ordinances and dismiss Polignac, but they were too late: Marmont was forced to abandon Paris to the mob, and the revolution was then all but over.

Though the worst of the violence lasted no more than three days, Charles did not believe the horror of it could be exaggerated.[2] There was fighting round the embassy, and the servants were forbidden to leave the building. Fortunately, however, Charles' wife and family were not there. Normal life came to a standstill and communications broke down. 'The interruption of the Posts and the difficulty in communication in Paris during the last three days render it impossible to give your Lordship satisfactory information respecting the events which have taken place', Charles reported to Aberdeen, in a dispatch dated 29 July, which he obviously hoped would get through all the same.[3] On 6 August he told Aberdeen that he had written to him every day since the barricades in the streets had been taken down, whether or not his dispatches had got through.[4]

Charles was much criticised then and on other occasions for the slackness of his reporting, in terms of regularity and clarity. It can be said on his behalf that the Foreign Office expected him to use the most economical methods of communication, and that he was not by any means the only ambassador of the time to be criticised for the opacity of his dispatches; but the reasons for his failure to keep in touch with the Foreign Office during this emergency are not clear. As it happened, there was a means of communication that was efficient and reliable, at least in normal times, apparently available to him. This was the Rothschilds' courier service, operated from a house outside Paris. Aberdeen made use of it, and in a letter dated 31 July he advised Charles to do so.[5]

Several political factions had started to vie for power as soon as the revolution began, but by 30 July the Chamber of Deputies was persuaded that Louis Philippe, Duc d'Orléans, should be offered the crown. The Chamber of Peers had little say in the matter. Charles and Louis Philippe had known each other since 1800, when Orléans and his two brothers, Beaujolais and Montpensier, exiled from France, had come to England. According to Violet Stuart Wortley, the three Princes visited the Stuarts' home near Christchurch in that year;[6] and, according to others, Louis Philippe took a house in Christchurch, if only briefly, in 1807.[7] They met occasionally in the years that followed,[8] and by this time Lady Louisa Stuart was able to describe them as 'good friends'.[9]

Events were moving quickly, and on that same day, 30 July, Louis Philippe sent a message to Charles from one of his houses in the country, asking for his advice. Should he accept the crown, or should he not? At this stage, Charles' instinct was sure. He reminded his friend that he had sworn an oath of loyalty to King Charles X, and advised him to stay where he was, away from Paris.[10] But, on 31 July, the Chamber of Deputies decided to offer him not the crown of France but the lieutenant-generalship of the kingdom, and he accepted it, informing the King that he had acted in what he believed to be the best interests of France.[11] Charles Stuart, reporting this development to Aberdeen, said he thought legitimacy – by which he meant the rights of the King and his heirs – had been preserved.[12]

Next, on 2 August, the King himself, who had moved to Rambouillet, sent to Charles for advice. Again, Charles acted shrewdly. He consulted his diplomatic colleagues, the Ambassadors of Austria, Prussia and Russia, and drew up a joint response. No advice could be offered, only the recommendation that His Majesty should look to his own safety and that of his family.[13] Advice or not, nothing could have been plainer than this and, later that day, the King abdicated in favour of his grandson, the Duc de Bordeaux, posthumous son of the Duc de Berri. At the same time, he announced that he intended to leave France, but a rumour had it that he would remain at Rambouillet until the accession of the Duc de Bordeaux, as Henry V, had been proclaimed, and this provoked another upsurge of anger among the people of Paris.

It was then that Charles made his first mistake, as far as Aberdeen and Wellington were concerned. When a mob formed in Paris early on 3 August, shouting for the blood of the Bourbons, he and Pozzo di Borgo went to the new Lieutenant-General of the kingdom and urged him to provide proper protection for the royal family at Rambouillet.[14] Louis Philippe assured them that he would do what he could, for the sake of his own name apart from any other consideration,[15] and there is no reason to believe he was not as good as his word. Charles had acted without instructions, however, and Aberdeen was to point out that more harm than good might have come of his intervention:

> Your interference under the circumstances mentioned in Your Excellency's Dispatch No. 387 when the personal safety of the King seemed to be seriously endangered was entirely consistent with the duties of your station as the representative of His Majesty. At the same time, it may be questionable if Your Excellency's intervention with the Duc d'Orléans had been generally known, whether it would have contributed to the security of the illustrious victim, or whether it might not rather have still further excited the hostile feelings of the populace.[16]

By the time Charles received this chiding, however, he had gone much further in what the Foreign Secretary and the Prime Minister could only interpret as 'interference'. It was clear on 3 August that the King, now the ex-King, would have to leave the country at once, and while the mob approached Rambouillet he set off for Cherbourg with his family, including the 9-year-old Duc de Bordeaux and the boy's mother, the Duchesse de Berri. But, before he left Rambouillet, he sent another message to Charles, with two specific requests. The first of these was that Charles should 'endorse a draft on Messrs. Coutts for the sum of six-hundred thousand francs',[17]

100

on behalf of the British government. Charles may have been saved from having to make a difficult decision about this by the Rothschilds, who are supposed to have stepped in with the amount in gold,[18] but he was so vague about it in his dispatches that for some time Aberdeen and Wellington could only guess at what he had done in the end.

The ex-Kings's second request was that Charles should inform him at once if any obstacle were put in the way of the Duc de Bordeaux's accession, and it was this that was to cause so much trouble. Charles was not an emotional man – Henry Brougham, who knew him well, once said he was 'buttoned up'[19] – but he was evidently moved, and he let Aberdeen know that he had been moved. The ex-King's messenger was waiting for a reply. 'I desired that person', said Charles, in the dispatch in which he reported the episode, 'to present my humble respects to His Majesty the King and to manifest my intention, at every risk, to comply with His Majesty's wishes'.[20]

Legitimacy was important to Charles, no doubt for a variety of reasons, including principle, pragmatism and the history of the Stuarts; and, if he had not felt it before, he now felt some personal loyalty to the ex-King. During the next two days, 4 and 5 August, he did his best to second-guess the outcome of the political infighting and horse-trading that was going on in Paris, and his difficulties were reflected in the series of letters that he wrote to Aberdeen at the time. In one, he argued that the Duc de Bordeaux's cause would be weakened if he left the country with his family,[21] and in another he warned that the young Prince's life would be in danger if he stayed in France.[22] He asked for Aberdeen's advice, specifically regarding the Duc de Bordeaux and he sent his letters to London, in a single batch, by one of his agents, a Mr Ivers.[23]

Then, on 6 August came the moment for which, in a sense, he had been waiting. In the Chamber of Deputies, the throne was declared vacant and Louis Philippe was named as its next occupant. No mention was made of the Duc de Bordeaux.

Without waiting any longer, either for Louis Philippe's response to the Chamber, which came the following day, or for Aberdeen's response to him, which was dated 8 August, Charles sent one of his staff, Colonel Hobart Cradock, secretly, to the ex-King. It was not generally known, either then or later, that Louis Philippe had recently offered to take charge of Bordeaux,[24,25] as if he was willing to safeguard his interests.

The first communication that Charles received from Aberdeen after having sent Cradock on his quixotic mission, dated 6 August, was in part a private letter in cipher and in part a public set of instructions. The letter gave the Foreign Secretary's response to Charles' appeal to Louis Philippe for the protection of the royal family on 3 August, which has already been quoted. The instructions must have made uncomfortable reading:

> His Majesty's Government are strongly impressed with the necessity not only of your abstaining from all interference, direct or indirect, in the proceedings of the various parties who have been called into action, but it is of almost equal importance that you should abstain from all expression of opinion.[26]

And they made the Foreign Secretary's response to Charles' request for advice as to what should be done about the Duc de Bordeaux, when it came, almost superfluous:

> It is not possible for me to take the responsibility of giving advice respecting the disposal of the Duke de Bordeaux. If the King should consent to leave him in France in consequence of this advice, it is to be feared that this alone would increase whatever danger might threaten him. That he could not remain without danger is certain; and yet it is equally certain that his stay in France offers

the best prospect of restoring the fortunes of this unhappy family. The situation of the King in this respect is the most difficult and cruel which can be imagined; but it is not foreign advice which can improve it.[27]

It was after having read the first of these missives that Charles had to compose an account of the mission for Aberdeen. He began with a sort of apologia:

Though I shall be careful to follow the course Your Lordship points out in your public despatch of the 6th August, circumstances had occurred before it came to hand, which induced me, under the impulse of a feeling I cannot think Your Lordship would disapprove, to over-step the limits it prescribes.[28]

He went on to describe those circumstances: the ex-King's requests of him, on 3 August, and the proceedings of the Chamber of Deputies on 6 August. He then came to the mission itself:

I therefore desired Colonel Cradock of this Embassy to follow the Court and to endeavour to see the King for the purpose of telling His Majesty the state of things, and to make known to him the language of the Duc d'Or-léans to the Russian Ambassador and myself respecting the Duc de Bordeaux, in order to enable His Majesty to judge how far it would be expedient to prevent the departure of the young Prince.
  Colonel Cradock returned a few hours before I received Your Lordship's despatch of the 6th August, and the accompanying report will show that without committing His Majesty's Government, he has obeyed my directions with intelligence and activity.
  As these proceedings though known to the Duc d'Or-

léans have not transpired, I flatter myself that the course I have pursued will not lead to inconvenience.

The votes of the Chambers, and the subsequent events in Paris having completely destroyed the hope of bringing forward the Duc de Bordeaux with any prospect of success, every consideration renders it expedient that he should now proceed to the asylum which may be chosen by the King and the other members of the Royal Family.[29]

Charles had acted impetuously. The royal party was travelling slowly, and would not reach Cherbourg for several days. If he had waited a single day he would have known that Louis Philippe had accepted the crown, thereby flouting the principle of legitimacy, so that there was no longer any question of his taking charge of the Duc de Bordeaux. Since this had always been one possible scenario, it was a pity that Louis Philippe had been let into the secret of Cradock's mission.

Cradock's report was enclosed. It gave a distinctly different impression of the mission:

I arrived at Merleroult, a league on this side of Nonant, at 10 o'clock on the night of the 7th, where I found the King in bed. I had no difficulty in being admitted to his presence when I stated to him the object of my journey, according to the instructions which I had received from Your Excellency. His Majesty said that he was most grateful to Your Excellency for communicating with him, and that you were the only person who had done so since his departure from Paris, or had sent him any information of the real state of affairs in the capital.

He felt that the question under consideration was a most important one, and he would endeavour to act for the best, but that he was proceeding to Cherbourg by the shortest possible journey, and would be still ten days or a fortnight in France, that he would during that time make up his mind as to what was to be done, but that I must feel how awful was his responsibility in thus being the arbiter of the fate, and perhaps existence of his grandson. He asked me if I was aware that the Duc d'Orléans had already refused to take charge of him, a proposition which he made, at the same time, with his deed of abdication: to whom then could he trust his child? His mother would never consent to abandon him, as she was persuaded that he would be poisoned if he were separated from the Royal Family. His Majesty said that he entirely admitted the soundness of the reasons urged by Your Excellency, but the difficulty, if not the impossibility of finding anyone to whom he could entrust the Duc de Bordeaux with safety made him hesitate to follow Your Excellency's counsel.

I told His Majesty that I thought the danger of the step was much exaggerated by parental affection, and that the presence of the legitimate heir to the throne was absolutely necessary for the encouragement of that Party, who were anxious and perhaps might finally be able to support his right, and I entreated His Majesty to give the subject his fullest consideration.

His Majesty said he would certainly do so, and as this was the most important point that could now occupy his mind he would give it his undivided attention.

I stated to His Majesty what Your Excellency had done with respect to the English men-of-war meeting him at Cherbourg, and the sum of money, for which you had applied in Your Excellency's letter to Lord Aberdeen. He seemed extremely grateful for this pecuniary supply, and he shook my hand violently when I told him of it.[30]

Charles had gone much further than he had cared to admit in his own account: he had advised the ex-King to leave the Duc de Bordeaux in France, and he had done so regardless of the changed situation created by Louis Philippe's acceptance of the crown.

Aberdeen passed both Charles' account and Cradock's report to Wellington, who responded angrily, on 13 August, before the outcome of the affair was known.[31] 'Lord Stuart was directed to keep himself clear of all interference', he began. 'What has he done under these orders?' he went on. Then he spelled it out. Lord Stuart had chosen from among his staff the man most likely to attract unwanted attention and sent him to the King, not only with information that he knew would make a delicate situation more delicate but also with gratuitous advice on the subject. His excuse was that he had made a promise to His Majesty, though he had not thought fit to mention this to his own government at the time.

Next, for Aberdeen's benefit, Wellington went deeper. Lord Stuart had advised the King to leave the Duc de Bordeaux in France as the symbol and personification of legitimacy, around whom supporters of legitimacy could rally; 'the only mode of prevailing upon people to declare in his favour'. He had been wrong to do so on two counts: first, circumstances alter cases, and though Louis Philippe had offered to take charge of the young prince he had no longer been willing or able to do so by the time Lord Stuart tendered his advice; but, secondly, and more to the point, whether or not the circumstances had changed, the advice should not have come from Lord Stuart.

Finally, as if Aberdeen did not know, Wellington pointed out why the advice should not have come from Charles:

We will suppose that the King follows this advice and leaves in France his grandson, and that there should be a party in his favour in consequence, and a civil war. Who will be responsible for it?

We may swear ourselves black in the face but nobody

will believe that we did not order Lord Stuart to take these measures to create this civil war.

But supposing what is more likely, that this prince should be poisoned or murdered. We shall be eternally disgraced.

Louis Philippe became King of the French on 9 August. The Duc de Bordeaux was not left in France, but arrived safely at Portsmouth, with his grandfather and his mother, on 17 August. Colonel Cradock's visit to the ex-King could not be kept a secret, but the reason for it did not become known until much later, when it had ceased to be of any importance. Wellington had expected to have to have Charles recalled, and Aberdeen warned him to be prepared for this blow, but sleeping dogs were let lie. Aberdeen was adept at deflecting questions, and his habit of corresponding privately with diplomats in the field tended to foil the inquisitive at the Foreign Office.

Colonel Cradock added a footnote to history at dinner with friends in 1848, by which time the death of his father had made him Lord Howden. The royal family was escorted to Cherbourg by loyal bodyguards, but also by so-called commissioners of the *de facto* government. According to Lord Howden, the commissioners had been instructed by Louis Philippe to oppose any scheme to leave the Duc de Bordeaux in France.[32]

15

The Rest 1831–1845

Charles' career was probably unaffected by his attempt to manipulate the French succession, if only because so few people knew about it. When, in November 1830, however, Wellington and Aberdeen were replaced as Prime Minister and Foreign Secretary, respectively, by Lord Grey and Lord Palmerston, Charles was replaced, again, as Ambassador at Paris by Lord Granville. He was to be given one more post, as Ambassador at St Petersburg, but that did not come until 1841, by which time he was already suffering from his last illness.

A loose end left hanging from his last year in France is the tantalising story of the Baronne de Feuchères.[1] She was born Sophie Dawes, in or about 1780, the daughter of an Isle of Wight fisherman. Sophie is unlikely to have been given much education, and went into service, but she evidently became an attractive and shrewd young woman who made a life for herself in the *demi-monde*. Eventually, in London, she was taken up by the Duc de Bourbon, Prince de Condé, a refugee from revolutionary and Napoleonic France, and when he was able to return to France, after the Restoration, she followed him. Her marriage to the Baron de Feuchères was a matter of convenience, arranged by her lover.

They may have been fond of each other at first, but he was an immensely wealthy man and she was an adventuress. It seems to be the case, too, that she was totally unscrupulous. Over the years, she manoeuvred herself into a position in which she could cow him and control his household, and it was said that he made his will to her dictation. By his will, the greater part of his property was to go to Louis Philippe's fourth son, the Duc d'Aumale, who was his godson; but a lesser part was to go to Sophie, and though it was a lesser part it was a fortune. There was a magnificent house in Paris, a great estate in the country and a large sum of money. But that was not all. The promise of the Duc d'Aumale's inheritance, it is said, ensured that she was received at the Court of Charles X, a prize that had so far eluded her.

Reporting the Duc de Bourbon's death, when it came, Charles referred to Sophie as 'the English lady who did his honours at the Palais Bourbon',[2] but there are few, if any, other references to her in his available papers, and we have no means of knowing how well he knew her. Violet Stuart Wortley, who had access to all his papers before they were dispersed, tells a story about Charles and Louis Philippe that may throw some light on the matter, but it may be no more than fiction. In this story, the two men discuss Sophie on the way to a party given by her, shortly before the revolution of 1830 that brought Louis Philippe to the throne:

'Tell me,' said Louis Philippe as they drove along, 'what do you know of the Baronne's antecedents?'

'The less you know, Altesse, the better,' Stuart replied. 'I have abstained from making too searching enquiries into the lady's past ...'[3]

Perhaps we are intended to believe that Charles knew more than he was prepared to say, since Mrs Stuart Wortley makes him go on to tell Louis Philippe almost all that we know now.

The Duc be Bourbon was found dead in his bedroom, hanging by his neck, on 27 August 1830. The findings of an early official enquiry were that he had committed suicide, in a state of depression due to the revolution of the previous month, but there was reason to believe that he had been murdered, and the finger of suspicion pointed at Sophie. She was never charged with any offence, perhaps because she had friends who could protect her, and Violet Stuart Wortley, in another of her stories that may or may not be based on fact, makes Charles tell Talleyrand, at a dinner at the embassy in September, that he has arranged for her to leave the country as quickly as possible.[4]

By this time, Charles had bought land near Christchurch, in Hampshire, and with it a house that he was to incorporate in the much grander building now known as Highcliffe Castle. He had no more use for his previous home, known successively as Bure Farm House, Bure Cottage and Bure Homage, at Mudeford, near Highcliffe, and when it was sold the purchaser was found to be the Baronne de Feuchères.[5] Charles and Sophie both employed the architect W.J. Donthorn on their new homes, and one architectural historian, writing about Donthorn's work, and aware that these two patrons, who had become each other's neighbours, had known each other in France, ventured what he called the 'art-historical speculation' that there was an illicit relationship between them.[6]

This piece of speculation has some superficial plausibility, and it might explain both Charles' reluctance to say much about Sophie to Louis Philippe – if there was any such reluctance – and his interest in getting her out of France when trouble loomed. But it is not supported by any evidence. Violet Stuart Wortley's hint that Charles knew more about Sophie than he should have done is not evidence, and if he arranged for her to leave France he was presumably doing his duty as British Ambassador. It is more to the point that Charles seems never to have bothered to suppress evidence of his amorous adventures, and it is also worth noting that there was no coincidence in Sophie's choice of a new home, since she had been born and brought up on the Isle of Wight, across the water from Mudeford.

In England, from 1831 to 1841, Charles divided his time between his home in London and his home in the country, 4 Carlton House Terrace and Highcliffe, but he was probably happier in town, where he had his clubs and his friends. He was a familiar figure at his clubs and at political dinners during the drama of parliamentary reform, the last scene of which was the passage of the Reform Bill of 1832. His two beautiful and talented daughters 'came out' and were married, the elder, Charlotte, to Charles Canning, George Canning's son, and the younger, Louisa, to the Marquess of Waterford. He had no son, but he was particularly fond of his nephew, another Charles Stuart.

Charles was a tireless traveller, and it was a family joke that one never knew where he would be off to next, or when he would reappear. He was always interested in foreign affairs, in Anglo-French relations and in matters private and secret. In the summer of 1840, relations between Britain and France were strained, and Wellington wrote in a letter to Lady Wilton:

Lord Stuart de Rothesay has returned from France. He has been at Cherbourg, Havre, Nantes, Rochelle, Bourdeaux [sic]. He says there never was anything equal to the animosity against the English everywhere. All are for war, even in these commercial towns.[7]

Fortunately, there was no war.

16

Postscript: The Rothschilds

The House of Rothschild established itself as a force to be reckoned with, financially and politically, in the early decades of the nineteenth century, when Charles Stuart was most actively engaged in diplomacy. The records show that Charles had dealings with the Rothschilds, chiefly while he was Ambassador at Paris, from 1815 to 1824 and from 1828 to 1830, and that some of those dealings may have been private and secret.

In 1994 the 1200th anniversary of the founding of the city of Frankfurt and the 250th anniversary of the birth in that city of the founder of the House of Rothschild, Mayer Amschel Rothschild, were marked by the publication of a set of essays, *The Rothschilds – A European Family*, edited by Georg Heuberger.[1] One of these essays provides a useful introduction to an account of the links between Charles and the second generation of the family, Mayer Amschel's five sons, Amschel, Salomon, Nathan, Carl and James. First, in a key statement about the rise of the House, we are told that 'the five brothers made their greatest profits after 1815 by speculating in bonds, by exploiting differences in quotations on the various exchanges and by conducting money transactions swiftly'.

The brothers relied for their success on being ahead of the game: as long as they knew before anyone else of events, or the prospect of events, that would influence the money markets of Europe they could buy or sell on the most favourable terms; and they knew about these things before anyone else because they were able to obtain accurate information and transmit it speedily. The means of obtaining accurate information and transmitting it speedily was much valued by men of power and influence in other spheres, and they were willing to share some of their power and influence in return for access to it. Thus, in addition to great wealth, the brothers acquired a degree of prestige and authority that wealth alone might not have brought them.

Information was obtained from 1800, or thereabouts, by a network of agents, connecting first Mayer Amschel and then his sons with the main financial, trading and political centres of Europe. The agents were recruited for their contacts and special knowledge, but though they had such qualifications in common they were otherwise a mixed collection of men and possibly women, including other bankers and businessmen, journalists and friends and relations of those in the know. The Rothschilds were by no means the only bankers or business-men to operate such a network, but they had no close competi-tors; and the same could be said of the communications system that they operated, about which there is more to come.

Heuberger shows that the year 1815 was as significant in the history of the House of Rothschild as it was in the history of Europe; and, as it happened, it was probably not until after Waterloo that Charles Stuart became aware of the importance of this new phenomenon on the financial and political scene. Tradition has it that Wellington was supplied with funds for his armies in the Peninsula in an audacious operation mounted by Nathan in England and James in France; but Charles was 'Wellington's right-hand man' in the Peninsula, and there is no reference to any such operation in his papers. The practical problems involved in funding Wellington's campaigns in the Peninsula were great, but there is no evidence that the Roths-childs contributed to their solution.

'Not until the beginning of 1814 is there any evidence of a connection between Nathan and Wellington's armies',

114

according to one of the historians of the House of Rothschild. 'Then, however, the evidence becomes abundant – and the connection was momentous'.[2] Wellington led his armies across the Pyrenees into France, and the Rothschilds kept him supplied, secretly, with enough money, in the form of French gold and silver coins, to support them until the war ended.[3] By this time, however, the partnership between Charles and Wellington had come to an end, and another partnership had become significant, that between Nathan and John Charles Herries, Commissary-in-Chief, who was ultimately responsible for Wellington's supplies.

Nathan and Herries worked together again in support of Wellington during the Waterloo campaign, while Charles was Ambassador at Brussels. Again, myth and legend have elaborated the story. It was one of the Rothschilds' most remarkable coups that Nathan obtained the news of victory before anyone else in England; but the claim that he made improper use of his special knowledge is false. The deals that he made at this time were not by any means spectacular, and – what is more – he and his brothers had overreached themselves, assuming that the war would last longer than, in fact, it did. The records give the impression that the Rothschilds, themselves, never knew exactly what their financial position was when the war ended.[4] It has also been suggested that Nathan bribed Marshal Grouchy to avoid the battle, but this is not credible.

The Rothschilds were immensely rich, and they used their wealth to establish themselves socially. They were assisted in their efforts when Napoleon was finally defeated by the honours that their services to the allied cause had brought them, particularly from Austria. It was not easy for them, however, because they were Jews and because they were considered uneducated. James, in Paris, a bachelor still, had been the most successful off them,[5] though even he was sometimes put down. Among the Rothschild Papers is a note from Charles' wife, Lady Elizabeth Stuart, as she was then, declining, in formal terms, an invitation to dinner one evening in the autumn of 1817.[6]

Whether or not the Stuarts and the Rothschilds knew each other socially by the autumn of 1817, Charles was certainly on business terms with James, and with Salomon, who had joined James in Paris. Several letters among the Rothschild Papers, written by James and Salomon to Nathan between October 1817 and February 1818, contain references to him, and though in some of them his name and title are not used in correct form the context makes it clear that they apply to him. Mentions of the Rothschilds in Charles' letters from these years are few and far between, however, and even as late as 1822, in a letter to Castlereagh, he referred to James as 'Mr Rothschild, the banker of this town', as if he had not had reason to refer to him in official correspondence before.[7]

Perhaps Charles' business with James and Salomon was still entirely unofficial. They made use of him, and he made use of them. They consulted him in their dealings with the French Government and over the affairs of Spain and Portugal,[8,9] and they reached Wellington through him.[10] They treated him particularly carefully at this stage; 'One cannot go and see people like that every day', Salomon told Nathan.[11] At the same time, they behaved like a spider with a fly. Charles apparently having told them that he enjoyed gambling, they gave him a share in one of their enterprises; and Salomon reminded Nathan of their father's dictum that 'when a Jew enters into partnership with a government official, he belongs to the Jew'.[12]

But it would be difficult to believe that Charles was ever in the Rothschilds' pocket; they certainly did not behave as if he was. When he wanted his financial dealings kept quiet in England, James asked Nathan to fix it: 'I owe this man a great deal and so if there is any way in which it can be done, please don't make difficulties'.[13] When Charles wanted a loan in

England and Nathan prevaricated, Salomon pointed out that they were dealing with the British Ambassador at Paris, a man of some importance, and that they depended on him for the success of certain negotiations in France.[14] James, too, pressed Nathan for a decision on the loan, which had first been mooted in 1817, writing to him in January 1818 with undisguised exasperation:

> It is really a circumstance extremely unpleasant to me that we are without any answer from you on the subject of the letter we forwarded to you from Sir Charles Stuart, as we are frequently in the habit of seeing him and consequently of being asked whether we have any information to give him. It makes us completely uncomfortable to be obliged always to answer in the negative and it must to him appear to arise *from neglect* on our part which you must be aware we are on every account most anxious to avoid as it relates to so considerable a sum to him as £12,000 stg. We must at least request, if you cannot procure a positive answer for him, that you will write us such a letter on the subject as we may show to him, if only to convince him of our desire of being serviceable to him and that we have not been unmindful of his request. You will really oblige us by attending to our desire, as we repeat we are almost ashamed to call on him till we are able to make him some communication.[15]

It would be interesting to know why Charles needed £12,000. He obviously did not need it in a hurry. One possibility is that he wished to add to his property in Hampshire.

The beginning of the Rothschilds' communications system was Nathan's regular correspondence with his father after 1798, when he left Frankfurt to settle in England; and an early development in it was an understanding between Nathan and

117

the seafaring communities of the Kent coast: 'At that time he became well known along the coast as a man who wanted the best service and was prepared to pay for it – handsomely. Generous bonuses were always available when Mr. Rothschild needed a brave captain to put to sea in bad weather'.[16] Later, he employed a firm of agents at Dover, 'a firm well equipped with light vessels ready to sail at a moment's notice with Rothschild despatches',[17] and 'post boys' as messengers on both sides of the Channel.[18]

The system grew as the brothers extended the range of their activities: Amschel, still at Frankfurt; Salomon, at Paris and then Vienna; Nathan, who took the lead in the family after Mayer Amschel's death in 1812, in London; Carl at Naples; and James in Paris. Eventually, there was a corps of couriers, described by Charles in 1830 as 'professional men on horse-back',[19] with what Talleyrand, at about the same time, said was a private ferry service across the Channel;[20] and they were ready for most – if not all – eventualities. On Christmas Day 1827, Salomon, in Vienna, found himself with important news for Amschel, at Frankfurt, and a courier ready to leave at once, but with no means of obtaining travel documents because all offices were closed.[21]

The Rothschilds were able to transmit information across Europe more quickly and reliably than were ministers in London or diplomats in the field, and this was particularly the case before 1824. Ministers and diplomats used either the public postal service or King's messengers, depending on the degree of security necessary, though ciphers provided extra security in the public postal system and correspondents might use their own servants as messengers. Transport for messengers was usually what was available to the public at large. Before 1824, King's messengers might have no particular qualifica-tions; in that year, Canning set certain standards: 'King's messengers were now to be British subjects, preferably former military or naval officers, who were over the age of thirty-five, competent in horse-riding and with facility in foreign languages'.[22]

No system was better than the Rothschilds', and it was widely used by others, Metternich, the Austrian Chancellor, in particular, for that reason. Castlereagh sanctioned its use, and Canning did so at first, when he succeeded Castlereagh, but he was well aware of the fact that it was not to be trusted. Canning's improvements to the King's messenger service in 1824 failed to provide him with a rival service, however, and the Rothschild couriers were still being used between Constantinople and London in 1825. In that year, the more or less blatant and systematic interference with dispatches in Vienna by Metternich's agents caused the Foreign Secretary to take countermeasures. Only approved messengers were to be used, and they were allowed to travel through Vienna but not to stay there.[23]

It has been said that, at this time, in the middle of the third decade of the nineteenth century, the Rothschilds were as unscrupulous as Metternich in the matter of the interception of letters,[24] and they certainly came under suspicion from Canning.[25] But, however unlikely it may seem to be, on *a priori* grounds, that they held aloof from so prevalent a practice, the evidence against them remains circumstantial. On the other hand, there is no doubt that they were regularly and as a matter of course obtaining influence and privileged information in return for financial favours,[26] and all their transactions of this sort took place at some point on a continuum between cooperation and corruption. If it is difficult to believe that Charles was ever in the Rothschild's pocket, his relationship with them might well have raised questions in Canning's mind.

Charles used the Rothschilds' courier service occasionally if not regularly. In January 1822, for example, he sent Sir William a'Court, British Minister at Naples, copies of dispatches that he had sent to Castlereagh, and he added a note: 'I avail myself of the departure of the Rothschild courier to send you the material dispatches which have been forwarded to London since the secret messenger from Naples passed through Paris'.[27] The background to this was that a revolution in Naples had been put down by Austria, and a revolution in Spain was attracting the attention of other governments.

Charles also used the Rothschilds' communication system as a source of information. In April 1822, information from James enabled him to assure Castlereagh that a crisis that was part of the Eastern Question had passed. War between Turkey and Russia had seemed imminent, but Salomon had had it from Metternich, who had had it from Tsar Alexander, that peace would be preserved.[28] Charles went on to inform Castlereagh, gravely, that Metternich had wished to be helpful to the House of Rothschild by passing this information to them, and he added, equally gravely, that the Austrian government had received a loan from the House of Rothschild soon afterwards.

It was in November 1823 that Herries, who had become Financial Secretary to the Treasury, wrote to Nathan, ostensibly at least on behalf of the Chancellor of the Exchequer, Frederick Robinson, to request a loan for Charles. What Herries told Nathan was that Charles needed between five and six thousand pounds for repairs to the embassy building.[29] But Nathan paid six thousand pounds into Charles' Special Account at Coutts, the account he used for his secret activities.[30] This may have been a ruse worked out between Herries and his friend, Nathan, to fund one of Charles' clandestine activities, presumably one that had been approved at a high level of government.

Charles had few contacts with the Rothschilds in the period 1824–1828, which separated his two terms as Ambassador at Paris. His second term was dominated by the revolution of 1830, when for several crucial days it was difficult, if not impossible, for him to communicate with the Foreign Office. Barricades and barriers, manned by revolutionaries, made it impossible for anyone to move about Paris except by foot,[31] and it is said that the revolutionaries did all they could to prevent diplomatic messengers from leaving the city.[32] The Foreign Secretary, now Lord Aberdeen, advised Charles to use the Rothschild couriers,[33] but this may not have been possible; Charles noted that the Rothschilds and other bankers were at their country houses,[34] as inaccessible to him as anywhere else outside Paris.

The revolution of 1830 was a shock and a surprise to the Rothschilds, though James had been given a hint of what might be to come.[35] It was not such a shock or surprise, however, that it prevented them from making a quick response. It was from the Rothschilds and not from Charles that Aberdeen learned of the insurrection. It was from the Rothschilds, too, that Metternich learned of it: 'It is remarkable evidence of the efficiency of the Rothschild news service, even during times of such disturbance', an early historian has pointed out, 'that both the British Government and the powerful Chancellor, who controlled the vast diplomatic machine of the Austrian Empire, should have received the first news of these important events from the House of Rothschild'.[36]

The Rothschilds looked for political stability in France, and they supported Charles X until it was clear that his day was done, when they eased his path to exile with gold and prepared to back Louis Philippe.[37] Their largesse incidentally relieved Charles Stuart of responsibility for the ex-King's succour, which he had so quixotically assumed on behalf of the British government.[38] But political stability was not to be bought, and France became a hotbed of intrigue and conspiracy again. There were Frenchmen working for a more far-reaching revolution, Belgians plotting against Holland, Neopolitan and Spanish exiles brooding over the state of their homelands and, no doubt, others, all fired by the events of the Three Glorious Days.

Some accounts have it that, in the face of the dangers of further cataclysms, the Rothschilds used their contacts and communication system as a quasi-political secret service;[39] but, once more, myth and legend have been at work.[40] What is true of this period, however, is that James had a close working relationship with Louis Philippe.[41] A series of letters in the Rothschild Archive, chiefly from Nathan's son Lionel in Paris to his parents in London,[42] shows that James now also had a close working relationship with Charles. And since Charles and Louis Philippe knew each other well, it is not difficult to imagine how useful each of the three might have been to the other two.

Charles' second term as Ambassador at Paris came to an end at the beginning of 1831, but he stayed on in the capital until the spring of that year. He stayed in touch with James and Lionel, too, and would discuss with them the affairs of the day, including his own. One day, in January, Lionel reported that the political and financial situation in Paris was confusing, and that what Charles had to say about it was 'generally partly true'; and he remarked of Charles that 'he never comes until the Exchange is over so that he can speculate on his news'.[43]

17

Epilogue

Charles Stuart was Ambassador at St Petersburg from 1841 to 1844, with a break in 1842 when he was given leave for Louisa's marriage and his friends were shocked by the obvious deterioration in his health. He was never well enough after this to carry out his duties, which were left to his staff, but he resisted having to resign for as long as he could. He spent the last year of his life at Highcliffe, with his wife, and died there in 1845; he had probably been suffering from cerebro-vascular disease. The funeral was held at the church that he had built at the gates of Highcliffe, now the parish church of St Mark, and it is recorded that he was buried in the vault, though new building has covered all signs of this. The only memorial to him is a tablet on the east wall of the chancel.

Though he was Ambassador at Paris twice, and for nearly ten years the first time, the most important of his acknowledged diplomatic achievements were the maintenance of the working relationship between Wellington and the Portuguese Regency Council, during the Peninsular War, and the negotiation of the treaty by which Brazil became independent of Portugal, in 1825. It is possible, of course, that his clandestine activities included other successes, which – because they were 'private and secret' – cannot be credited to him.

Notes

Chapter 1

1 *Dictionary of National Biography*
2 Ellis
3 Andrew, p. 2
4 Gudgin, p. 12
5 Parritt, p. 28
6 Stuart Wortley (1), p. 170
7 BL. Add.MSS.38222, ff. 98–122
8 Stuart Wortley (2), p. 31
9 Stuart Wortley (1), p. 279
10 TNA(PRO). WO.1/297, f. 1
11 Stuart Wortley (1), p. 180
12 Charles Stuart's journal (1)
13 Stuart Wortley (1), p. 270
14 Charles Stuart's journal (2)
15 Ibid., p. 109

Chapter 2

1 Atherton (1), p. 7
2 Ellis, p. 60 et seq.
3 Atherton (1), p. 7
4 Sparrow (1), p. 368
5 Ibid.
6 Sparrow (2), p. 307
7 Sparrow (1), p. 370
8 Atherton (2), p. 41
9 Bindoff, p. 12
10 Hobart Papers. D/MH/H(War Office)/S
11 Stuart Wortley (2), p. 24 note
12 Hobart Papers. D/MH/H(War Office)/S, M12
13 Ibid., M20
14 Ibid.

15   Ibid.
16   Ibid., M21
17   Ibid., M18
18   EUL Dk.6.25/1
19   Nicolas, v.5, p. 169
20   Hobart Papers. D/MH/H(War Office)/S, M.15
21   Ibid., M20
22   Home, p. 187
23   Letter from Elizabeth Sparrow
24   Ibid.
25   Arch.Nat. F76384
26   ESRO. WST.5/11a
27   Rose (1), v.1, p. 453
28   Ibid., p. 455
29   Sparrow (2), p. 276
30   TNA(PRO). FO.7/69
31   Ibid.
32   Ibid.
33   Rose (1), v.1, p. 454
34   Home, p. 181
35   NLS. MS.6244
36   Machado

Chapter 3

1   Bindoff, p. 110
2   Hinde, p. 166
3   Rose (2), p. 713
    Sparrow (2), p. 362
4   Rose (2), p. 713
5   Stapleton (1), p. 125
    Hinde, p. 171
6   Anon, p. 349
7   Rose (1), v.2, p. 135 and p. 136 note
8   Hinde, p. 171
9   Ibid.
10   Rose (1), v.2, p. 140
11   Rose (2), p. 178
12   Anon, p. 349
13   Hinde, p. 171

14   ESRO. AMS.6297/15
15   Letter from Barbara Abbs
16   ESRO. ACC.5640/7/3
17   Abbs, p. 162
18   Granville, v.2, p. 227
19   Historical Branch, LRD, p. 4
20   Malmesbury (1), v.4, p. 393
21   Canning Papers. WYL250/GC/59a
22   BL. Add.MSS. 41542
23   Duckworth, p. 211
24   Ibid., p. 293

Chapter 4

1   Stuart Wortley (2), p. 109
2   Carr, p. 80
3   TNA(PRO). FO.72/57
4   Charles Vaughan's journal
5   Stuart Wortley (2), p. 134 note
6   Ilchester (1) p. 400
7   TNA(PRO). FO.72/57
8   Ibid.
9   Ilchester (1), p. 400
10   TNA(PRO). FO.72/57
11   Ibid.
12   Ibid.
13   Ibid.
14   TNA(PRO). FO.72/58
15   TNA(PRO). FO.72/59
16   Oman, p. 526
17   Stuart Wortley (2), p. 161
18   Ilchester (1), p. 418
19   Stuart Wortley (2), p. 119
20   Ibid., p. 141
21   Ibid., p. 156
     Bruce, p. 43

Chapter 5

1   Aspinall (1), v.5, p. 98

2   Malmesbury (2), v.1, p.161
3   Parritt p. 46
4   Ibid., p. 47
5   Haswell, p. 124
6   Longford (1), p. 211
7   Ibid., p. 212
8   TNA(PRO). KV.1/1, p. 21
9   Sparrow (2), p. 382
10   Gurwood (1837), v.6, p. 427
11   Stuart Wortley (2), p. 170
12   Page, p. 173
13   Aspinall-Oglander, p. 239
14   Broughton, p. 3
15   Stuart Wortley (2), p. 184
16   Ibid., p. 185 note and p. 209 note
17   Gurwood (1837), v.5, p. 536
18   Rousseau, p. 103
19   Wellington Papers, WP1/327/31
20   Ibid., WP1/330/18
21   Gurwood (1852), v.4, p. 583
22   Ibid., v.4, p. 586
23   Ibid.
24   Ibid., v.4, p. 583
25   Wellington Papers, WP1/330/31
26   Page, p. 57
27   ESRO. ACC.5640/7/3
28   Ibid., AMS.6297/15
29   Gurwood (1837), v.6, p. 53
30   Rosselli, pp. 66 & 67
31   Bentinck Papers, Pw.Jd.5093
32   TNA(PRO). FO.342/43

Chapter 6

1   NLS. MS.6161, f. 485
2   Stuart Wortley (2), p. 226
3   Ibid.
4   Webster (1), p. 448
5   Ibid., p. 547
6   Gudgin, p. 14

7   Haswell, p. 222
8   Maxwell, p. 236
9   Chandler, p. 149
10 Ferguson, p. 16
11 ESRO. AMS.6297/15

Chapter 7

1   Cooper, p. 284
2   Pilbeam, p. 18
3   NLS. MS.6171
4   Ibid.
5   Ibid.
6   Temperley, p. 271
7   NLS. MS.6225
8   Leveson Gower, v.1, p. 67
9   Longford (2), pp. 34 & 48
10 NLS. MS.6207
11 NLS. MS.6192
12 Ibid.
13 Ibid.
14 NLS. MS.6214
15 NLS. MS.6176
16 NLS. MS.6171
17 NLS. MS.6175–6179 & MS.6182 & 6183
18 NLS. MS.6196
19 Ibid.
20 Daudet, p. 75
21 Mansel, p. 331
22 NLS. MS.6217
23 NLS. MS.6189
24 Ibid.
25 Daudet, p. 67
26 Ibid.
27 NLS. MS.6244
28 BL. Add.MSS.43082, f. 66
29 Daudet, p. 67
30 NLS. MSS.6188
31 Stuart Wortley (2), p. 255
32 NLS. MSS.6203

33   Stuart Wortley (2), p. 265
34   Ibid., p. 266
35   Coutts
36   NLS. MSS.6165–6195
37   Sparrow (2), p. 44
38   *Dictionary of National Biography*
39   Ibid.
40   Sparrow (2), p. 40
41   Ibid.
42   Ibid, pp. 54 & 55
43   Ibid., p. 54
44   BL. Add.MSS.41533
45   Medlam, p. 80

Chapter 8

1   Hall, p. 141
2   Glover, p. 152
3   Bruce, p. 43
4   Stuart Wortley (2), p. 101
5   Ibid., p. 122
6   Bruce, p. 181
7   BL. Add.MSS.30120, ff. 323–327
8   BL. Add.MSS.30121, ff. 9 & 10
9   NLS. MSS.6166
10   Lewis, v.3, p. 94
11   NLS.MS.6172
12   Ibid.
13   NLS. MS.6168
14   Ibid.
15   Ibid.
16   Ibid.
17   Ibid.

Chapter 9

1   *Confidential Friend of the Departed*
2   Tomalin, p. 302
3   Longford (2), p. 34

4   NLS. MS.6172, f. 331
5   Tomalin, p. 303
6   *Dictionary of National Biography*
7   NLS. MS.6177
8   Tomalin, p. 257
9   NLS. MS.6172, f. 503

Chapter 10

1   NLS. MS.6197
2   NLS. MS.6203
3   Ibid.
4   NLS. MS.6201
5   NLS. MS.6204
6   NLS. MS.6201
7   NLS. MS.6204
8   NLS. MS.6201
9   Fraser, p. 280
10 Pilbeam, p. 23
11 NLS. MS.6171
12 Hansard, 1822, v.6, col. 1430
13 Wellington Papers, WP1/758/32
14 NLS. MS.6217
15 Wellington Papers, WP1/789/10
16 Ibid.
17 NLS. MS.21289, f. 75
18 ESRO, AMS.6297
19 Coutts, Separate Account, 1823–1824, p. 741
20 RAL X1/T6/32
21 Letter from the Director, the Rothschild Archive, London

Chapter 11

1   TNA(PRO). FO.360/4
2   Temperley, p. 271
3   TNA(PRO). FO.360/3
4   Stuart Wortley (3), p. 196
5   BL. Add.MSS.41549, ff. 10 & 11
6   Ibid., f. 52

7 TNA(PRO). FO.360/3
8 Ibid.
9 Ibid.
10 Canning Papers, WYL250/GC/109
11 BL.Add.MSS. 41549, ff. 8 & 9
12 Ibid., f. 152
13 Stapleton (2), v.2, p. 19
14 BL. Add.MSS.41549, f. 26
15 Ibid., f. 21
16 Stuart Wortley (2), p. 185 note
17 Ibid., p. 209
18 Ibid.
19 Wellington Papers, WP1/895/20
    Maxwell, p. 486
20 Bindoff, p. 51

Chapter 12

1 Chamberlain, p. 8
2 Ibid., p. 9
3 Bindoff, p. 51
4 BL. Add.MSS.43082, ff. 27 & 28
5 Ibid., ff. 33 & 34
6 Ibid., ff. 29 & 30
7 NLS. MS.6214
8 BL. Add.MSS.43082, ff. 33 & 34
9 Ibid, ff. 98 & 99
10 EUL. Dk.6.25/29
11 Wellington Papers, WP1/1111/32
12 BL. Add.MSS.43082, ff. 92 & 93
13 Ibid., ff. 66 & 67
14 NLS. MS.6244

Chapter 13

1 BL. Add.MSS.43083, f. 124
   NLS. MS.6239, f. 655
2 Wellington Papers, WP1/971/8
3 NLS. MS.6234, f. 405

4　NLS. MS.21298, f. 75
5　Abbs, p. 163
6　Ibid.
7　Ibid., p. 161
8　NLS. MS.6239, f. 625
9　BL. Add.MSS.43083, f. 124
　　NLS. MS.6239, f. 655
10　Home, p. 189
11　NLS. MS.6238 f. 215
12　Ibid., f. 245
13　Wellington Papers, WP1/1054/58
14　Letter from Barbara Abbs
15　NLS. MS.31306, ff. 108 & 109
16　Abbs, p. 169
17　Ibid., p. 163
18　Will of William Wood
19　Ibid.

Chapter 14

1　Gontaut, v.2, p. 152
2　Home, p. 224
3　NLS. MS.6242
4　Ibid.
5　BL. Add.MSS.43085, ff. 70–72
6　Stuart Wortley (3), p. 203
7　Woodward, v.3, p. 107
8　Hare, v.1, p. 265
　　Stuart Wortley (2), p. 227
9　Home, p. 224
10　NLS. MS.6242, f. 393
11　Ibid., f. 425
12　Ibid.
13　Ibid., f. 459
14　Ibid., f. 495
15　Ibid.
16　NLS. MS.6245, f. 555
17　NLS. MS.6242, f. 637 et seq.
18　Chamberlain, p. 239
19　Maxwell, p. 210

20 NLS. MS.6242, f. 637 et seq.
21 Ibid., f. 505
22 Ibid., f. 517
23 BL. Add.MSS.43085, ff. 93–95
    Chamberlain, p. 239
24 Nicoullaud, v.3, p. 314
25 NLS. MS.6242, f. 644
26 NLS. MS.6245, f.555
27 BL. Add.MSS.43085, ff. 93–95
28 NLS. MS.6242, f. 637
29 Ibid.
30 NLS. MS.6242, f. 643 et seq.
31 Wellington Papers, WP1/1137/43
32 Chancellor, v.2, p. 299

Chapter 15

1 Bowen
2 NLS. MS.6243
3 Stuart Wortley (3), p. 201
4 Ibid., p. 205
5 Ibid.
6 O'Donnell, p. 87
7 Wellington, p. 136

Chapter 16

1   Heuberger, p. 85
2   Davis, p. 30
3   Ibid., p. 31
4   Ferguson, p. 109
5   Corti, p. 204
    Ferguson, p. 207
6   RAL. X1/T17/65
7   NLS. MS.6212
8   RAL. X1 /109/8
9   Ibid.
10 RAL. X1/109/9
11 RAL. X1/109/8

12 Ibid.
13 RAL. X1/109/9
14 RAL. X1 /109/9/1/82
15 RAL. X1/109/9/1/3
16 Wilson, p. 43
17 Cowles, p. 47
18 Ibid.
19 BL. Add.MSS.43085, f. 87
20 Corti. p. 425
21 RAL. X1/T5/239
22 Jones, p. 117
23 Temperley, p. 268
24 Cowles, p. 71
25 Temperley, p. 268
26 Ferguson, pp. 163–172
27 BL. Add.MSS.41533, f. 209
28 NLS. MS.6212
29 RAL. X1/T6/32
30 Coutts
31 NLS. MS.6242
32 Chamberlain, p.238
33 BL. Add.MSS.43085, ff. 70–72
34 Ibid., f. 87
35 Ferguson, p. 229
36 Corti, p. 427
37 Ferguson, p. 248
38 NLS. MS.6242, f. 637 et seq.
39 Cowles, p. 82
40 Ferguson, p. 248
41 Ibid., p. 233
42 RAL. X1/T17 series
43 RAL. X1/T17/127

Bibliography

Manuscript Sources and Abbreviations

Arch.Nat.   Archives Nationales, Paris.
Bentinck Papers   Papers of Lord William Bentinck. Hallward Library, University of Nottingham.
BL   British Library, London.
Canning Papers   Papers of George Canning. Leeds District Archives, West Yorkshire Archive Service.
Charles Stuart's journal (1)   *Travels in Germany and the Hereditary States, 1795–1797*. Lord Joicey.
Charles Stuart's journal (2)   *Travel Journal, Northern Europe, 1801*. Bodleian Library, University of Oxford. MS. Eng. misc. c. 256.
Charles Vaughan's journal   *Journal of Travels in Spain, 1808*. Codrington Library, All Souls College, Oxford.
Coutts   Charles Stuart's Accounts, Coutts & Co, London.
ESRO   East Sussex Record Office, Lewes.
EUL   Edinburgh University Library
Hobart Papers   Papers of Robert Hobart, Baron Hobart. Buckinghamshire Record Office, Aylesbury.
NLS   National Library of Scotland, Edinburgh.
RAL   The Rothschild Archive, London.
TNA (PRO) The National Archives (PRO), Kew.
Wellington Papers   Papers of the 1st Duke of Wellington. Hartley Library, University of Southampton.

Published Sources

Abbs, Barbara. A Maresfield entrepreneur. *Sussex Archaeological Collections*, Vol. 132 (1994), 161–172.
Andrew, Christopher. *Secret Service: The Making of the British Intelligence Community*. William Heinemann Ltd., London, 1985.
Anon. Canning and the Treaty of Tilsit. *The Edinburgh Review*, Vol. CC111 (1906), No. CCCCXVI, 345–361.

Aspinall (1), A. (Ed.) *The Later Correspondence of George III.* Cambridge University Press, 1970.

Aspinall (2), A. (Ed.) *The Letters of King George IV 1812–1830.* Cambridge University Press, 1938.

Aspinall-Oglander, Cecil. *Freshly Remembered: The Story of Thomas Graham, Lord Lynedoch.* The Hogarth Press, London, 1956.

Atherton (1), Louisa. *Top Secret: An Interim Guide to Recent Releases of Intelligence Records at the Public Record Office.* Public Record Office, Kew, 1993.

Atherton (2), Louisa. *'Never Complain, Never Explain': Records of the Foreign Office and State Paper Office 1500–c.1960.* Public Record Office, Kew, 1994.

Bindoff, S.T., Malcom Smith, E.F. and Webster, C.K. (Eds) *British Diplomatic Representatives 1789–1852.* The Royal Historical Society, London, 1934.

Bowen, Marjorie. *The Scandal of Sophie Dawes.* John Lane, London, 1935.

Broughton, S.D. *Letters from Portugal, Spain and France, Written During the Campaigns of 1812, 1813 and 1814.* Longmans, Hurst, Rees, Orme, and Brown, London, 1815.

Bruce, Ian. *Lavalette Bruce.* Hamish Hamilton, London, 1953.

Carr, Raymond. *Spain 1808–1839.* Oxford University Press, 1966.

Chamberlain, Muriel E. *Lord Aberdeen: A Political Biography.* Longman Group Ltd, London, 1993.

Chancellor, E. Beresford. (Ed.) *The Diary of Philipp von Neuman 1819–1850.* Philip Alan & Co., Ltd, London, 1928.

Chandler, David. (Ed.) *Napoleon's Marshals.* Weidenfeld & Nicolson, London, 1987.

Confidential Friend of the Departed. Public and Private Life of that Celebrated Actress Miss Bland, otherwise Mrs Ford or Mrs Jordan. J. Duncombe, London, ND.

Cooper, Duff. *Talleyrand.* Phoenix (Orion Books Ltd), London, 1997.

Corti, Count. *The Rise of the House of Rothschild.* Victor Gollancz Ltd, London, 1928.

Cowles, Virginia. *The Rothschilds: A Family of Fortune.* Weidenfeld & Nicholson, London, 1973.

Daudet, Ernest. (Ed.) *La Police Politique.* Plon-Nourrit et Cie, Paris, 1912.

Davis, Richard. *The English Rothschilds.* William Collins, London, 1983.

Duckworth, Colin. *The D'Antraigues Phenomenon.* Avero Publications Ltd, Newcastle-upon-Tyne, 1986.

Ellis, Kenneth. *The Post Office in the Eighteenth Century.* Oxford University Press, 1958.

Ferguson, Niall. *The World's Banker: The History of the House of Rothschild.* Weidenfeld & Nicolson, London, 1998.

Fraser, Flora. *The Unruly Queen.* Papermac, London, 1997.

Glover, Michael. *A Very Slippery Fellow: The life of Sir Robert Wilson 1777–1849.* Oxford University Press, 1977.

Gontaut, The Duchesse de. *Memoirs of.* Translated by Mrs J.W. Davis. Chatto & Windus, London, 1894.

Granville, Castalia, Countess. (Ed.) *Lord Granville Leveson Gower (First Earl Granville): Private Correspondence.* John Murray, London, 1916.

Gudgin, Peter. *Military Intelligence: A History.* Sutton Publishing Ltd, Stroud, 1999.

Gurwood, Lieut-Colonel. (Ed.) *The Dispatches of Field Marshal the Duke of Wellington.* John Murray, London, 1837 and 1852.

Hall, John R. *The Bourbon Restoration.* Alston Rivers Ltd, London, 1909.

Hansard, *Parliamentary Debates.*

Haswell, Jock. *The First Respectable Spy: The Life and Times of Colquhoun Grant, Wellington's Head of Intelligence.* Hamish Hamilton, London, 1969.

Heuberger, Georg. (Ed.) *The Rothschilds – A European Family.* Boydell and Brewer Ltd, Woodbridge, 1994.

Hinde, Wendy. *George Canning.* William Collins, London, 1973.

Historical Branch, L.R.D. *F.C.O. Records: Policy, Practice and Posterity 1782–1993.* (No. 4 in the *History Notes* series produced by the Library and Records Department of the Foreign and Commonwealth Office, second edition, revised in 1993.)

Home, The Hon. James A. (Ed.) *Letters of Lady Louisa Stuart to Miss Louisa Clinton.* Second Series. David Douglas, Edinburgh, 1903.

Ilchester (1), The Earl of. (Ed.) *The Spanish Journal of Elizabeth Lady Holland.* Longmans, Green & Co., London, 1910.

Ilchester (2), The Earl of. (Ed.) *The Journal of the Hon. Edward Fox (afterwards fourth and last Lord Holland) 1818–1830.* Thornton Butterworth Ltd, London, 1923.

Jones, Raymond A. *The British Diplomatic Service 1815–1914.* Colin Smythe, Gerrards Cross, 1983.

Leveson Gower, The Hon. F. (Ed.) *Letters of Harriet Countess Granville 1810–1845.* Longmans, Green & Co., London, 1894.

Lewis, Lady Theresa. (Ed.) *Journals and Correspondence of Miss Berry.* Longmans, Green & Co., London, 1866.

Longford (1), Elizabeth. *Wellington – The Years of the Sword.* Weidenfeld & Nicolson, London, 1969.

Longford (2), Elizabeth. *Wellington – Pillar of State.* Weidenfeld & Nicolson, London, 1972.

Machado, Cândido Guinle de Paula. (Ed.) *Charles Landseer: Sketchbook Containing Studies made in Brazil 1825–1826* and Associated Papers. Printed privately. São Paulo, 1972.

Malmesbury (1), The Third Earl of. (Ed.) *Diaries and Correspondence of James Harris, First Earl of Malmesbury.* Richard Bentley, London, 1844.

Malmesbury (2), The Earl of. *Memoirs of an Ex-Minister.* Longmans, Green & Co., London, 1884.

Mansel, Philip. *Louis XVIII.* Sutton Publishing Ltd, Stroud, 1999.

Maxwell, Sir Herbert. (Ed.) *The Creevey Papers.* John Murray, London, 1923.

Medlam, Sarah. *The Bettine, Lady Abingdon Collection.* The Victoria and Albert Museum, London, 1996.

Nicolas, Sir Nicholas. (Ed.) *The Dispatches and Letters of Vice-Admiral the Lord Viscount Nelson.* Henry Colburn, London, 1844–1846.

Nicoullaud, M. Charles. (Ed.) *Memoirs of the Comtesse de Boigne.* William Heinemann, London, 1907.

O'Donnell, Roderick. W.J. Donthorn (1799–1859): Architecture with 'great hardness and decision in the edges'. *Architectural History,* Vol. 21 (1978), 24–31.

Oman, Carola. *Sir John Moore.* Hodder & Stoughton, London, 1953.

Page, Julia V. *Intelligence Officer in the Peninsula: Letters and Diaries of Major The Hon. Edward Charles Cocks 1786–1812.* Spellmount Ltd, Tunbridge Wells, 1986.

Parritt, B.A.H. *The Intelligencers: The History of British Military Intelligence up to 1914.* Intelligence Corps Association, Templer Barracks, Ashford, 1983.

Pilbeam, Pamela. *The Constitutional Monarchy in France 1814–48.* Longmans, Harlow, 2000.

Roper, Michael. *The Records of the War Office and Related Departments 1660–1964.* Public Record Office, Kew, 1998.

Rose (1), J. Holland. *The Life of Napoleon 1.* G. Bell & Sons, London, 1910.

Rose (2), J. Holland. A British Agent at Tilsit. *The English Historical Review*, Vol. XVI (1901), 712–718.

Rosselli, John. *Lord William Bentinck: The Making of a Liberal Imperialist 1774–1839.* University of California Press, Berkeley and Los Angeles, 1974.

Rousseau, I.J. (Ed.) *The Peninsular Journal of Major-General Sir Benjamin D'Urban 1808–1817.* Longmans, Green and Co., London, 1930.

Sparrow (1), Elizabeth. The Alien Office. *The Historical Journal*, Vol. 33, 2 (1990), 361–384.

Sparrow (2), Elizabeth. *Secret Service. British Agents in France 1792–1815.* Boydell & Brewer Ltd, Woodbridge, 1999.

Stapleton (1), Augustus Granville. *George Canning and His Times.* John W. Parker & Son, London, 1859.

Stapleton (2), Edward J. (Ed.) *Some Official Correspondence of George Canning.* Longmans, Green & Co., London, 1887.

Stuart Wortley (1), Violet. *A Prime Minister and His Son.* John Murray, London, 1925.

Stuart Wortley (2), Violet. *Highcliffe and the Stuarts.* John Murray, London, 1927.

Stuart Wortley (3), Violet. *Magic in the Distance.* Hutchinson and Co., Ltd., London, 1948.

Temperly, Harold. *The Foreign Policy of Canning 1822–1827.* G. Bell & Sons Ltd., London, 1925.

Tomalin, Claire. *Mrs Jordan's Profession: The Story of a Great Actress and a Future King.* Viking, London, 1994.

Webster (1), Sir Charles. *The Foreign Policy of Castlereagh 1812–1815.* G. Bell & Sons Ltd., London, 1931.

Webster (2), Sir Charles. *The Foreign Policy of Castlereagh 1815–1822.* G. Bell & Sons Ltd., London, 1931.

Wellington, The 7th Duke of. (Ed.) *Wellington and His Friends.* Macmillan, London, 1965.

Wilson, Derek. *Rothschild: A Story of Wealth and Power.* André Deutch, London, 1994. (Revised edition.)

Woodward, B.B., Wilks, Theodore C. and Lockhart, Charles. *A General History of Hampshire.* Virtue & Co., London, 1861–1869.

Index